W9-AGA-163

THE ENCYCLOPEDIA OF HOMEMADE DIPS

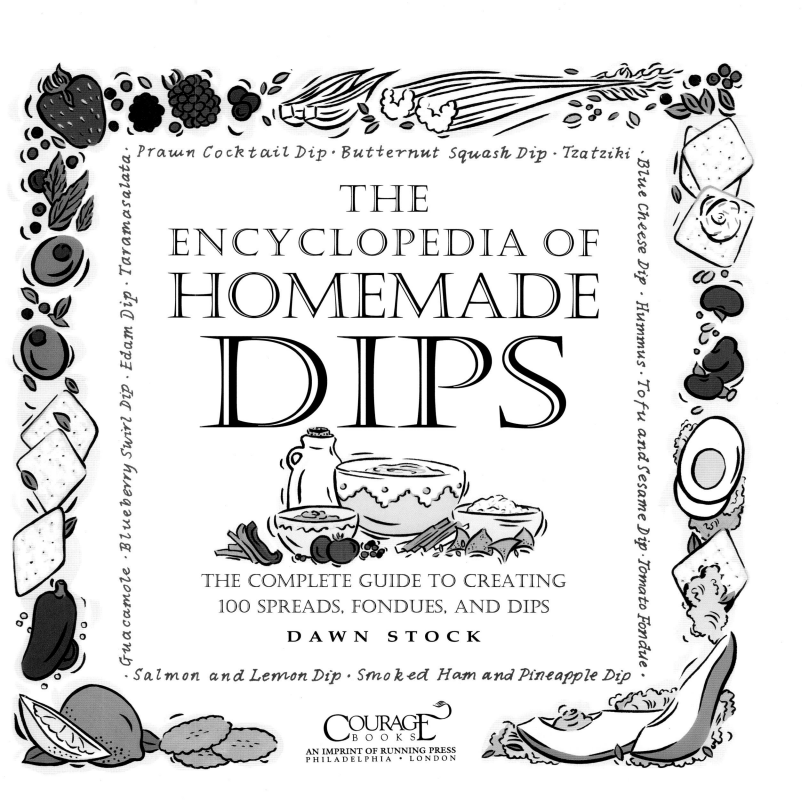

Prawn Cocktail Dip · Butternut Squash Dip · Tzatziki ·

THE ENCYCLOPEDIA OF HOMEMADE DIPS

THE COMPLETE GUIDE TO CREATING
100 SPREADS, FONDUES, AND DIPS

DAWN STOCK

Blue Cheese Dip · Hummus · Tofu and Sesame Dip · Tomato Fondue

Guacamole · Blueberry Swirl Dip · Edam Dip · Taramasalata ·

· Salmon and Lemon Dip · Smoked Ham and Pineapple Dip ·

COURAGE BOOKS

AN IMPRINT OF RUNNING PRESS
PHILADELPHIA · LONDON

A QUINTET BOOK

© 1996 by Quintet Publishing Limited

All rights reserved under the Pan-American
and International Copyright Conventions
First published in the United States of America
in 1996 by Running Press Book Publishers

Printed in Singapore by
Star Standard Industries (Pte) Ltd

This book may not be reproduced in whole or
in part, in any form or by any means,
electronic or mechanical, including
photocopying, recording or by any information
storage or retrieval system now known or
hereafter invented, without written permission
from the publisher and copyright holder.

9 8 7 6 5 4 3 2 1

Digit on the right indicates the number
of this printing

ISBN 1-56138-629-4

Library of Congress
Cataloging-in-Publication Number
96-67165

This book was designed and produced by
Quintet Publishing Limited
6 Blundell Street
London N7 9BH

Creative Director: Richard Dewing
Designer: Ian Hunt
Project Editor: Diana Steedman
Editor: Amy Boaz Nugent
Illustrator: Joanne Makin

Typeset in Great Britain by
Central Southern Typesetters, Eastbourne
Manufactured in Singapore by
Universal Graphics Pte Ltd

Published by Courage Books, an imprint of
Running Press Book Publishers
125 South Twenty-Second Street
Philadelphia, Pennsylvania 19103-4399

Contents

Introduction

This collection of recipes was put together with a lot of enjoyment since all of the different dips tested and devised have such a wide variety of flavors and textures there was never a chance for the taste buds to get bored. The majority of dips included here are very quick and easy to make, which make them ideal foods for the trend toward snacking rather than eating set meals. However, this is not an endorsement of the "grazing" style of eating, and I still believe that taking time out to sit down and enjoy good food and company properly makes us happier and healthier folk.

The cookbook is conveniently divided into eight, covering the different dips: cheese, fish, poultry and meat, vegetables, bean and lentil, fruit (savory and sweet), fondues (savory and sweet), and more favorites with a final section containing "at a glance" tables of all 100 dips and their serving suggestions that you can browse through (or maybe even dip into) for inspiration.

But first, before you start cooking, here's just a few words about the various types of dips included, a few helpful preparation and serving tips, some ideas and hints on preparing the accompaniments, and the cook's notes to help make your life in the kitchen easier.

TYPES OF DIPS

There is certainly more to the culinary world of dips than just a bowl of chilled yogurt and a few strips of raw vegetables, and that's without starting to think about all the different types of foods that can be served with a dip. Dips can be savory or sweet, cooked or uncooked, served hot or cold.

Many consider the fondue the ultimate dip. You'll learn more about fondue techniques at the beginning of the fondue chapter. Throughout the book, you will find dips covering all the above possibilities.

Dips are no new thing; we have probably been dipping into our foods since we evolved. In the early days, when there were no plates or eating implements, what better way of scooping up your food than with other vegetables, fruits and bread. Throughout the world, there are national favorite dips and this book includes a selection of the most popular and well known, such as hummus and tzatziki from Greece, guacamole from Mexico, tapenade from Spain, raita and dals from India, and dips from China and Thailand.

The popularity of dips may be due to the fact that there is something satisfying and familiar about dipping your finger into a sauce when cooking, or, when we were younger, being allowed to clean out the chocolate frosting bowl. Maybe dips are an adult way in which we can indulge ourselves in this satisfying way of eating.

WHEN TO SERVE DIPS

Dips tend to be an informal way of eating, which in itself adds to their enjoyment and makes them ideal for serving to family, and friends, or even as a treat when by yourself. Most of us probably think of serving dips at parties or as a first course at a dinner; however, dips can be served at any time of the day, from a wholesome brunch (see Creamy Egg Brunch Dip, page 68 – ideal for when you have guests for the weekend or at a working breakfast), to snacks any time of the day, light lunches, and packed lunches, first courses, main meals, desserts, suppers, at parties and when entertaining (see Scarlet Delight Dip for Halloween, page 35, and Cranberry and Orange Dip for serving at Thanksgiving or Christmas, page 52). We don't need an excuse when to dip – we can treat ourselves any time, even when watching television or reading.

HOW TO SERVE DIPS

No strict rules apply as to how to serve dips, since they tend to be informal and generally need no special serving equipment. Special fondue sets and forks can be purchased, which add fun to the occasion, but I find keeping the fondue warm on a tabletop warmer with nightlights just as effective.

All you need is a suitable serving bowl to serve the dip in, or individual ramekin dishes and plates or bowls in which to arrange the variety of dipping accompaniments. Unusual containers in which to serve your dip can liven up your table setting. Hollow out a crusty loaf or individual bread rolls to make an unusual, edible bowl. Fruits and vegetables can also be hollowed out and filled with a dip. Pineapples, large tomatoes, eggplants, bell peppers, and squash all make great serving containers. A crab dip looks stunning if served in cleaned crab shells.

PREPARATION IN ADVANCE

Many dips actually benefit from being made well in advance so that they have several hours chilling time in order for the flavors to mingle and mature. The exceptions tend to be dips made with fresh fruit which exude natural juices, making the dip too moist if chilled for too long, and fondues which are best made and served immediately. If a dip benefits from several hours chilling time or requires serving soon after being made, a recommendation has been made in that particular recipe.

The consistency of the dips throughout the book vary greatly, from fairly thin to a thick and hearty spread. Some are smooth, others crunchy, and the salsas are made from small diced vegetables and fruits that require substantial accompaniments with which to scoop up the chunky pieces.

Dips made with cream cheese, sour cream and yogurt tend to thicken upon chilling, so before serving, stir the dip to soften its texture sufficiently. However, if you find your dip still a little too thick, simply stir in one to two tablespoons of milk before transferring it to a serving dish.

Many vegetables used as raw dipping accompaniments can be prepared several hours in advance, then placed in an airtight container and kept in the refrigerator. Carrots, celery, zucchini, cucumber, crisp lettuce leaves, broccoli and cauliflower florets, strips of colorful bell peppers, trimmed scallions, fennel, and endive are all suitable for advance preparation. However, quartered button mushrooms are best prepared just before serving to prevent discoloration, tomato wedges become too wet if left to stand in their own juices, and onion wedges and rings are best prepared just prior to serving because their strong odor may taint other foods in the refrigerator.

Some vegetables are better used for dipping after they have been cooked very slightly. These can be prepared well in advance, drained, and left to chill in the refrigerator. Baby sweet corn, fine green beans, snow peas, and asparagus tips are particularly good once cooked and chilled. The cooking time entails little more than blanching. Trim the vegetables if necessary and bring a pan of water to a boil. Add the vegetables, return the pan to a boil, and simmer for no more than one to two minutes so that the vegetables are still crunchy. Drain in a colander and cool with cold running water, drain well, and store in the refrigerator.

Deep-fried, batter-coated vegetables can be partially prepared in advance. The batter (see page 28 for recipe) can be made and chilled until required and the vegetables chopped into bite-sized pieces and chilled in an airtight container until they need coating and cooking.

Fruits used for dipping are best prepared not too far in advance because they can become wet if left in their own juices. Some fruits, for example apple, pears, bananas, and peaches, discolor when cut open. To help prevent fruit from discoloring and browning, the fruit can be dipped in lemon, lime, or orange juice immediately after slicing and then arranged on a serving plate.

THINGS FOR DIPPING

It is important to stress that you need to use the best quality and freshest produce available. There is nothing worse than trying to scoop up a dip with a limp piece of carrot or lettuce leaf past its prime. Vegetables should be crisp and crunchy with a fresh color, while fruits should be ripe, but not overripe and certainly not bruised. Even if the vegetables and fruits are to be served barbecued, broiled, or batter-coated and fried, they still need to be of the best quality.

Many vegetables tend to be cut into strips, called sticks or crudités. Don't make the strips too long or else you end up with too much vegetable and too little dip, and there's a temptation to redip after you've taken a bite. Too short and the vegetable, and your fingers, get covered in dip as you scoop. Both of these are no problem if you're eating by yourself, but may not impress your guests. I find cutting the vegetable strips to about two inches long ideal.

Pears, apples, peaches, nectarines, papayas, mango, and melons are best served in small wedges, with their skins removed, cored or deseeded as required. Bananas can be served in sticks and soft fruits such as seedless grapes, strawberries, and raspberries can be hulled and left whole. You may find it helpful to use small forks or cocktail sticks for picking up the fruit and dipping.

Fish, meat, and poultry can be served cut into bite-sized nuggets. Strips of batter- or crumb-coated fish, meat, and poultry are also sometimes called *goujons*, which adds a certain classiness to your dip, particularly if you're entertaining to impress. Use tender and lean cuts that will stay tender after quick cooking, as broiling, stir frying, and deep frying are ideal cooking methods for fast accompaniments to dips.

Many batter- or crumb-coated bite-sized meat and poultry products now exist in the supermarkets and make fine accompaniments to dips. However, it can be fun to make your own individual accompaniments and you can refer to the batter- and crumb-coated turkey recipes on page 28 and 52. These coatings can also be used other meats or fish and the batter used on vegetables and fruits as well.

There are many other foods suitable for dipping, see the charts on pages 70–79, plus you will have your own personal discoveries. However, below are a few more ideas to spark your imagination and taste buds.

The ever-increasing selection of breads available from bakeries and supermarkets make ideal accompaniments – they are economical, tasty, and filling. They are also easy to prepare, requiring only to be sliced or cubed. Bread can also be toasted, made into croutons, garlic bread, and melba toast. Don't forget the special breads as well, such as pita, bagels, and flavored breads such as olive, tomato, rye, and pumpernickel.

Breadsticks, crackers, potato chips, tortilla chips, nachos, shrimp and rice crackers all add different tastes and textures to the meal as accompaniments to dips.

And for those of you with a sweet tooth, I'm sure you'll find it hard to resist the selection of sweet fondues and fruit dips. Dipping marshmallows, mini cookies, mini doughnuts, and cubed cake into Autumnal Fruits with Port Dip or Devil's Chocolate Fondue is simply delicious.

ARE DIPS HEALTHY?

As with most things – there is the good and the bad! Some dips can be considered extremely healthy, low in calories, fat, sugar, and salt, while others are laden with fat, sugar, and calories. However, this book contains a selection of both so there should be something to suit everyone's diet and lifestyle.

Some of the dips could be considered very righteous because they are low in fat and salt and when served with plenty of raw vegetables or fruit and crusty bread make a nutritious snack or meal. Others can be made "healthier" for those of you counting the calories or fat content by using the lower fat alternatives such as lowfat/reduced calorie mayonnaise, yogurt, or cream cheese. However, some of the dips were just meant to be rich and there's no reason why most of us shouldn't treat ourselves occasionally.

Remember, it's not just the dips that should be considered, it's often the foods we choose to dip them with that can make the most difference. Choose healthier dipping options such as raw fruit and vegetables, delicious by themselves, rather than the batter-coated and fried varieties. Use fruit instead of cakes, cookies, and marshmallows. A selection of cubed crusty brown and white breads are delicious and filling and healthier than dipping chips and other salty fried snack foods.

But most important, if possible don't just snatch a meal or snack: these dips are quick and easy to prepare so take a little time out to enjoy some good food either by yourself or in the company of family and friends.

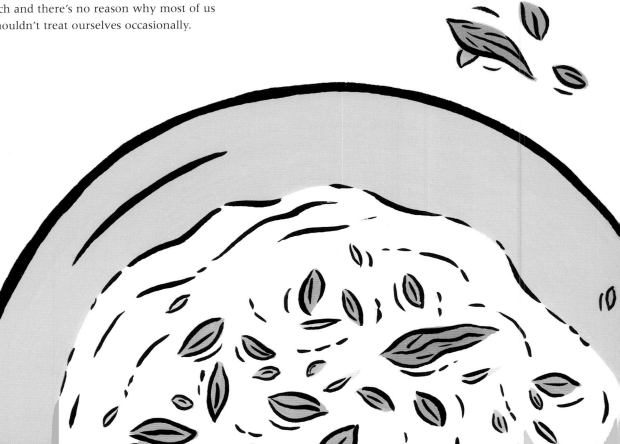

HOW MANY PEOPLE DO THE DIPS SERVE?

Portions depend on when and how you intend to serve the dip. If you are serving the dip at a buffet party with lots of other foods, then the dip will serve considerably more than when eaten by itself. I find it is better to serve several different dips at a buffet rather than making vast quantities of just one dip. Make sure you have plenty of dipping accompaniments nearby.

However, as a general guideline the dips that make one and one-quarter to one and one-half cups will serve about four to six people as a starter or first course and about two to three people as a main course when served with plenty of dipping accompaniments.

The dips that make two to two and one-half cups will serve about eight to twelve as a starter and four to six people as a main meal.

A little of your own judgment and knowing your guest's appetites will help determine serving quantities and how much food you will need as dipping accompaniments. I have always found that it is best to provide more than you think you'll need, particularly with fondues, since there is a great temptation when sitting and chatting to dip and dip, again and again!

COOK'S NOTES

Please take a few moments to read these notes before starting to make any of the recipes.
1. The quantities made by the dips are approximate guidelines and are given to help you assess how much you will make and how many people it will serve to suit your requirements.
2. Cooking times are given as a guideline, but may vary with different ovens. Helpful hints on what to look for at the cooked stage have been given in the recipes to ensure you get the best results.
3. All spoon measurements are level spoonfuls.
4. All eggs used are medium-size eggs.
5. Freshly ground black pepper has been used to season many of the dips. Salt has rarely been added, but do season to your own taste.
6. Some of the recipes require the chopping and deseeding of fresh chiles. If you are unfamiliar with handling chiles, take care to wash your hands and utensils thoroughly after cutting them. If you prefer a hot chile flavor there is no need to remove the seeds since they contain a lot of the chile's fiery heat.
7. The Garlic Dip and Creamy Egg Brunch Dip contain raw or soft-boiled eggs. Note that eggs should not be consumed raw or lightly cooked by people at risk, such as those with weak immune systems and pregnant women. The other recipes use hard-boiled eggs, which are fully cooked and can be safely consumed by those considered at risk.
8. The ingredients used in the dips need to be stored in the refrigerator for safety and hygiene. Where the recipes say chill, it is important to use the refrigerator for this purpose.

CHEESE
DIPS

4

Ricotta and Cream Walnut Dip

MAKES ABOUT 1½ CUPS

The Italian cheese Ricotta has a very mild, smooth, creamy flavor, so the pieces of walnut add a crunchy bite.

9 oz Ricotta
5 Tbsp heavy cream
½ cup shelled walnuts, chopped
4 Tbsp fresh parsley, chopped
Freshly ground black pepper
Strips of celery, apple wedges, and bagels

1. Soften the Ricotta with the heavy cream in a bowl until smooth and well combined.
2. Stir the chopped walnuts into the dip, reserving a few for garnish. Add the parsley. Season to taste with freshly ground black pepper. Cover and chill.
3. Turn the dip into a serving bowl and garnish with the reserved walnuts. Serve with celery sticks, cored apple wedges (dipped in lemon juice to prevent discoloring), and bagels cut into bite-sized pieces.

Beer and Cheddar Dip

MAKES ABOUT 1½ CUPS

A "ploughman's lunch" all in a dip! Use a sharp cheddar to complement the beer.

½ cup sharp cheddar cheese, grated fine
7 oz cream cheese
3 fl oz beer
Freshly ground black pepper
Trimmed scallions, potato chips, and breadsticks

1. Soften the cream cheese in a bowl and stir in the cheddar.
2. Gradually blend in the beer and season the dip with freshly ground black pepper. Cover and chill.
3. Transfer the dip to a serving bowl. Serve with scallions, a selection of chips and breadsticks.

Green Olive and Cream Cheese Dip

MAKES ABOUT 2 CUPS

This hearty dip is ripe with flavor and quite a feast when served with breadsticks and warmed strips of pita bread.

7 oz lowfat cream cheese
⅓ cup low-calorie mayonnaise
7 oz pitted green olives
2 scallions, chopped fine
Freshly ground black pepper
Breadsticks and pita bread, cut into strips

1. Blend the cream cheese and mayonnaise in a mixing bowl.
2. Reserve five olives for a garnish and place the remaining olives in a small blender and process for a few seconds until chopped but not completely smooth.
3. Add the processed olives and chopped scallions to the cheese mixture and mix thoroughly. Season to taste with freshly ground black pepper. Spoon into a serving dish and garnish with olive rings cut from the reserved olives. Cover and chill.
4. Serve with breadsticks and strips of warmed pita bread.

Cheese and Pimento Dip

MAKES ABOUT 1¼ CUPS

If possible, use freshly grated Parmesan rather than the ready-grated variety for a full-flavored dip.

¼ cup Parmesan, grated fine
¼ cup sharp cheddar cheese, grated fine
1 cup drained canned pimentoes
A few drops of hot sauce
Breadsticks and potato and tortilla chips

1. Mix together the Parmesan and cheddar cheeses in a bowl.

2. Place the pimentoes in a blender or food processor and process for a few seconds until smooth. Mix the puréed pimentoes with the cheese and season to taste with a few drops of hot sauce. Cover and chill.

3. Transfer the dip to a serving bowl and serve with breadsticks and potato and tortilla chips.

Brie and Pear Dip

MAKES ABOUT 1½ CUPS

This dip is best served fairly soon after making in order to enjoy the flavor of the pear. It becomes masked by the brie on keeping.

1 ripe pear
½ cup plain yogurt
5 oz brie cheese
Freshly ground black pepper
Small wedges of cantaloupe and watermelon, skin and seeds removed

1. Peel and core the pear. Chop coarsely and place in a blender or food processor with the yogurt. Process for a few seconds until smooth.
2. Add the brie in chunks and process until smooth. Season well with freshly ground black pepper. Place in a serving dish, cover and chill.
3. Serve the dip with small wedges of cantaloupe and watermelon.

Pistachio and Blue Cheese Dip

MAKES ABOUT 1¼ CUPS

Simply delicious is the verdict for this dip and a firm favorite in my house. The pistachios add a wonderful crunchy texture to the creamy rich dip.

4 oz blue cheese
⅔ cup plain yogurt
3 Tbsp milk
3 oz pistachios, roasted in their shells
Freshly ground black pepper
Crusty bread, strips of celery and wedges of crisp apple

1. Crumble the blue cheese finely into a bowl with the back of a fork.
2. Stir in the yogurt and enough milk to make a coating dip. Mix well.
3. Shell the pistachios and rub off any excess husk and skin where possible. Coarsely chop the nuts, reserving a few for garnish. Stir the chopped pistachios into the dip, cover, and chill.
4. Spoon the dip into a serving dish and garnish with the reserved chopped pistachios. Serve with small chunks of crusty bread, strips of celery, and cored apple wedges (dipped in lemon juice to prevent discoloring).

Smoked Cheese Dip

MAKES ABOUT 1¼ CUPS

The smoked flavor matures and gets stronger the longer this dip is chilled.

5 oz smoked processed cheese, for example Austrian, rind removed
1 cup mayonnaise
1 tsp Dijon mustard
Freshly ground black pepper
Toasted cubes of bread, a selection of crackers, tomato wedges, and cucumber strips

1. Break the cheese into chunks and place in a blender or food processor with the mayonnaise and mustard. Process for a few seconds until smooth.
2. Spoon into a bowl and season with freshly ground black pepper. Cover and chill.
3. Transfer the dip to a serving bowl. Serve with toasted cubes of bread, a selection of crackers, tomato wedges, and strips of cucumber.

Dill, Yogurt, and Cream Cheese Dip

MAKES ABOUT 1¼ CUPS

The sweet, slightly aniseed flavor of dill makes this dip a wonderful accompaniment to fennel, endive, and cucumber crudités.

7 oz lowfat cream cheese
⅔ cup lowfat plain yogurt
3 Tbsp fresh dill, chopped
1 tsp lemon juice
Freshly ground black pepper
Fresh dill sprigs
Lemon slices
Strips of fennel, endive, and cucumber

1. Soften the cream cheese in a mixing bowl with a spoon. Blend in the yogurt to form a smooth consistency.
2. Stir the chopped dill into the yogurt mixture along with the lemon juice.
3. Season to taste with freshly ground black pepper. Cover and chill.
4. To serve, transfer the dip to a serving bowl, garnish with dill sprigs and slices of lemon. Serve with vegetable crudités of fennel, endive, and cucumber. This dip is also well suited to serve with deep-fried batter- or crumb-coated strips of fish.

Peppercorn Cheese Dip

MAKES ABOUT 1¼ CUPS

If possible, use mixed white, green, and black peppercorns for varying colors and strengths to add flavor and interest to the dip. Use freshly grated Parmesan, not the ready-grated variety available at the grocery store – the flavor is 100 times superior.

7 oz cream cheese
4 Tbsp Parmesan, finely grated
4 Tbsp milk
3 Tbsp mixed whole peppercorns (white, green, and black)
Breadsticks, cheese straws, strips of cucumber and carrot

1. Soften the cream cheese in a bowl and stir in the Parmesan.
2. Add the milk gradually to the cheese mixture to make a smooth dip.
3. Lightly crush the peppercorns in a pestle and mortar. Alternatively place the peppercorns in a small plastic bag and gently roll a rolling pin over the bag to crush the peppercorns. Take care not to overcrush the peppercorns since it is best if the dip has a slightly crunchy texture.
4. Stir the peppercorns into the cheese dip mixture, cover, and chill.
5. Spoon the dip into a serving dish and serve with breadsticks, cheese straws, and strips of cucumber and carrot.

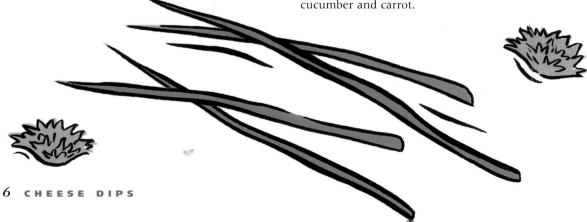

Mountain High Dip

5 oz goat cheese
⅔ cup heavy cream
1 oz fresh mixed herbs (e.g. parsley, chives, oregano, thyme)
Freshly ground black pepper
Chunks of crusty bread and hearty strips of celery, cucumber, and carrot

1. Soften the goat cheese in a bowl with the back of a fork.

2. In a separate bowl, lightly whip the cream to a soft, dropping consistency.

3. Remove any large or woody stalks from the herbs and chop the leaves very finely. Mix the cream and herbs into the softened goat cheese. Season to taste with freshly ground black pepper. Cover and chill.

4. Spoon the dip into a serving dish and serve with chunky pieces of crusty bread and hearty strips of celery, cucumber, and carrot.

Cream Cheese and Chive Dip

Delicate chives are more subtle in flavor than raw onion and using low-calorie alternatives helps make this dip a healthier option for those of you watching your fat intake or counting calories.

7 oz lowfat cream cheese
3 Tbsp low-calorie mayonnaise
4 Tbsp skim milk
1 tsp Dijon mustard
3 Tbsp fresh chives, chopped
Freshly ground black pepper
Fresh chive flowers (if in season)
Red onion wedges, celery, carrot, bell pepper strips

1. Soften cream cheese in a mixing bowl with the mayonnaise and milk until smooth.

2. Stir in the mustard and chives, reserving some for garnish. Season to taste with freshly ground black pepper. Cover and chill.

3. To serve, spoon into a serving bowl and garnish with remaining chopped chives or chive flowers. Serve with red onion wedges and strips of celery, carrot, and bell peppers.

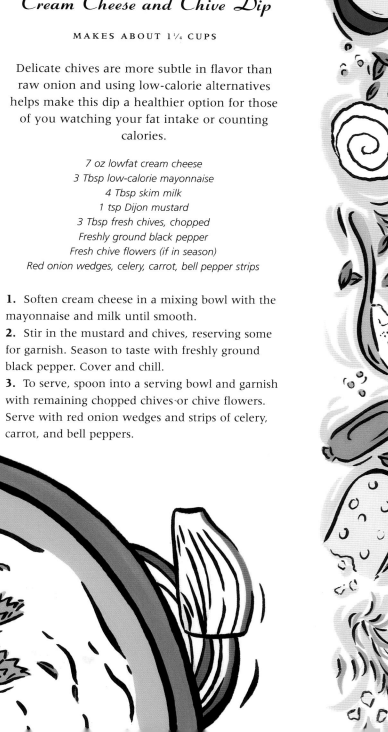

Blue Cheese Dip

MAKES ABOUT 2 CUPS

This dip can take strong-flavored crudités such as cauliflower and broccoli. The longer it chills in the refrigerator, the more the flavor develops.

5 oz strong blue cheese, e.g. Danish Blue
1¼ cups sour cream
2 Tbsp celery leaves, chopped fine
Freshly ground black pepper
Strips of celery and small florets of cauliflower and broccoli
Celery leaves to garnish

1. Crumble the blue cheese finely into a mixing bowl with a fork.
2. Add the sour cream and celery leaves reserving some leaves for garnish. Mix thoroughly. Season to taste with freshly ground black pepper. Cover and chill.
3. To serve, turn the dip into a serving bowl and garnish with celery leaves. Serve with raw strips of celery and small florets of cauliflower and broccoli.

Edam Dip

MAKES ABOUT 1¼ CUPS

If you can find a small whole Edam, carefully cut off the top and hollow out the cheese so that it can then be used as a container in which to serve your dip.

1 cup Edam, finely grated
½ cup plain lowfat yogurt
3 Tbsp low-calorie mayonnaise
2 pinches of paprika
Freshly ground black pepper
Quartered button mushrooms, tomato wedges, broccoli florets, and sticks of carrot

1. Mix the grated Edam with the yogurt and mayonnaise in a bowl.
2. Add a pinch of paprika and season well with freshly ground black pepper. Cover and chill.
3. Spoon the dip into a serving bowl or hollowed cheese and sprinkle with a pinch of paprika to garnish. Serve with raw quartered button mushrooms, tomato wedges, broccoli florets, and carrot sticks.

Cottage Cheese and Caper Dip

MAKES ABOUT 2 CUPS

Capers have a Mediterranean flavor and colorful bell pepper crudités complement this dip well, adding a sunny appearance.

1 cup cottage cheese
3 Tbsp capers, chopped
⅔ cup sour cream
1–2 Tbsp milk
1 scallion, chopped fine
Freshly ground black pepper
Strips of red, green, yellow bell peppers and raddichio leaves

1. Place the cottage cheese in a small mixing bowl, add the capers and sour cream, mixing thoroughly. If the mixture is a little too thick, add some of the milk.
2. Stir in the scallion, reserving some for garnish.
3. Season to taste with freshly ground black pepper. Spoon the mixture into a serving dish, sprinkle with the reserved chopped scallion, cover, and refrigerate.
4. Serve with strips of colorful peppers and raddichio leaves. This dip can also be served with strips of deep-fried batter- or crumb-coated fish.

FISH
DIPS

2

Creamy Caviar Dip

MAKES ABOUT 1½ CUPS

Creating a dip is one way of making a little caviar go a long way. If you cannot find real caviar, use lumpfish caviar instead.

⅔ cup heavy cream
1 Tbsp shallot, chopped very fine
1 lemon, with rind grated very fine
3½ oz jar caviar or lumpfish caviar
Freshly grated black pepper
Melba toast

1. Lightly whip the cream to a soft dropping consistency. Stir in the shallot, lemon rind, and all but two teaspoons of the caviar. Season to taste with freshly ground black pepper. Cover and chill.
2. Spoon the dip into a serving dish and garnish with the reserved caviar. Serve with melba toast.

Caper and Tartar Dip

MAKES ABOUT 1½ CUPS

This dip is ideal to serve with warm strips of crumb- or batter-covered white fish such as cod, haddock, or hoki that have been baked or deep fried.

2 oz small gherkins, plus enough for garnish
1 Tbsp capers
1 cup mayonnaise
1 Tbsp lemon juice
1 tsp white wine vinegar
2 Tbsp fresh parsley, chopped
1 Tbsp fresh chives, chopped
Freshly ground black pepper
Bread-crumb or batter-coated fish strips or nuggets, strips of bell peppers, and crisp lettuce leaves

1. Finely chop the gherkins and capers, reserving slices of gherkins for garnish.
2. Combine all of the ingredients together in a bowl. Season to taste with freshly ground black pepper. Cover and chill.
3. Transfer the dip to a serving bowl and serve with warm deep-fried or oven-baked fish strips, strips of raw bell peppers and crisp lettuce leaves.

Quick Anchovy Dip

MAKES ABOUT 1¼ CUPS

This speedy dip is packed with flavor.

2 oz canned anchovies in olive oil, drained
7 oz cream cheese
1 medium onion, chopped
1 garlic clove, crushed (optional)
1 Tbsp lemon juice
Freshly ground black pepper
1 Tbsp fresh chives, chopped
Green and black pitted olives, quartered button mushrooms, strips of bell pepper, and chunks of Ciabatta or olive bread

1. Place the anchovies, cream cheese, onion, garlic, and lemon juice in a blender or food processor and process for a few seconds until smooth.
2. Turn the mixture into a bowl and season to taste with freshly ground black pepper. Cover and chill.
3. Spoon the mixture into a serving dish and garnish with chopped chives. Serve with pitted green and black olives, quartered button mushrooms, strips of bell pepper, and chunks of bread, preferably Italian Ciabatta or olive bread.

Smoked Mackerel and Horseradish Dip

MAKES ABOUT 1½ CUPS

Smoked mackerel and horseradish – both strong flavors made for each other.

5 oz smoked mackerel fillets, skin and bones removed
⅔ cup plain yogurt
3 Tbsp creamed horseradish sauce
1 Tbsp lemon juice
Freshly ground black pepper
Sprigs of parsley and lemon slices
Triangles of toasted white and brown bread

1. Break the fish into chunks and place in a mixing bowl. Carefully remove any small bones you may find.

2. Using the back of a fork, mash the fish into a paste consistency. Stir in the yogurt, horseradish sauce, and lemon juice. Season to taste with freshly ground black pepper. Cover and chill.

3. Spoon the dip into a serving bowl and garnish with sprigs of parsley and lemon slices. Serve with warm triangles of toasted white and brown bread.

Creamy Tuna Dip

MAKES ABOUT 1½ CUPS

7 oz canned tuna in water or oil, well drained
½ cup low-calorie mayonnaise
¼ cup lowfat plain yogurt
½ small lemon, juice and rind, grated fine
2 anchovy fillets
Freshly ground black pepper
Sprig of fresh parsley
Strips of celery, cucumber, baby sweetcorn, and tomato wedges

1. Place tuna in a mixing bowl. Using a fork, flake the fish into fine even pieces.

2. Stir in the mayonnaise, yogurt, lemon juice and rind.

3. Chop the anchovy fillets into small pieces and mash with the back of a fork on a small plate. Add to the dip.

4. Season to taste with freshly ground black pepper. Place in a serving bowl, cover, and chill.

5. Garnish the dip with fresh parsley. Serve with strips of celery and cucumber, cooked and cooled baby sweetcorn, and tomato wedges.

Smoked Salmon and Lemon Dip

MAKES ABOUT 1¼ CUPS

This is an excellent dip served as a first course.

2 oz smoked salmon
7 oz cream cheese
3 Tbsp milk
1 lemon
1 Tbsp fresh dill, chopped fine
Fresh ground black pepper
Sprigs of dill and lemon slices
Melba toast, strips of cucumber, celery, and carrot

1. Finely chop the smoked salmon. Soften the cream cheese in a bowl with the milk.

2. Finely grate the rind of the lemon. Add the rind and juice of the lemon to the softened cheese and mix together with the chopped salmon and dill. Season to taste with freshly ground black pepper. Cover and chill.

3. Spoon the dip into a serving bowl and garnish with sprigs of dill and lemon slices. Serve with melba toast, cucumber, celery, and carrot.

Thai Coconut and Chile Crab Dip

MAKES ABOUT 1¼ CUPS

Thai food has a wonderful fresh appearance and flavor – tempt your tastebuds with this dip.

⅔ cup heavy cream
1 oz shredded coconut
6 oz canned white crab meat, well drained
2 scallions, chopped fine
1 Tbsp fresh coriander, chopped fine
2 Tbsp lime juice
1 red chile, deseeded and chopped fine
Freshly ground black pepper
Fresh coriander leaves
Rice and shrimp crackers, trimmed scallions, strips of red bell pepper, cucumber, and carrot

1. Place the cream and coconut in a small saucepan. Slowly bring the cream almost to a boil, then remove from the heat, stir, and leave to infuse for ten minutes.

2. Strain the cream through a fine sieve into a bowl, pressing the coconut with a back of a spoon. Discard the coconut collected in the sieve. Leave the cream to cool completely.

3. Place the crab meat in a bowl and break apart into small pieces with a fork. Stir in the cooled cream, scallions, chopped coriander, lime juice, and chile. Season well with freshly ground black pepper. Cover and chill.

4. Transfer the dip into a serving dish and garnish with coriander leaves. Serve with rice and shrimp crackers, trimmed scallions, and strips of red bell pepper, cucumber, and carrot.

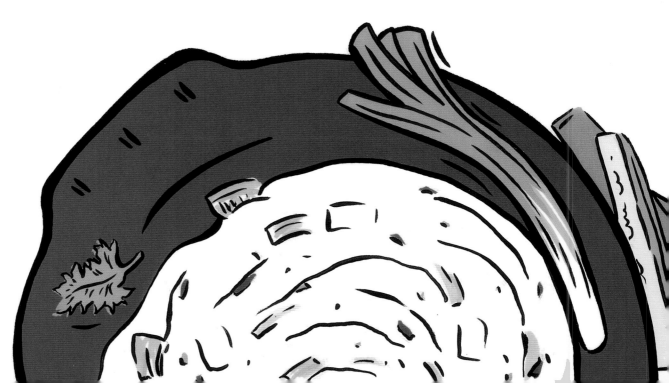

Deviled Egg and Tuna Dip

MAKES ABOUT 1¼ CUPS

Make this dip as fiery as you wish by adding as
much hot sauce as you can handle.

2 hard-boiled eggs
3½ oz canned tuna in water or oil, drained
⅔ cup mayonnaise
2 scallions, chopped fine
A few drops of hot sauce
Freshly ground black pepper
Tortilla chips, toasted garlic bread, and strips of celery

1. Remove the egg shells and chop the eggs very
finely.
2. Mash the tuna with the back of a fork in a
bowl. Add the egg, mayonnaise, and all but one
tablespoon of the chopped scallion. Mix
thoroughly.
3. Add sufficient hot sauce to taste and season
well with freshly ground black pepper. Cover and
chill.
4. Turn the dip into a serving dish and garnish
with the reserved chopped scallion. Serve with
spicy tortilla chips, toasted garlic bread, and strips
of celery.

Chive and Smoked Oyster Dip

MAKES ABOUT 1¼ CUPS

*2 3½ oz cans smoked oysters in oil, well drained (you
require about 6 oz drained weight of oysters)*
2 Tbsp fresh chives, chopped
⅔ cup sour cream
Freshly ground black pepper
Melba toast

1. Reserve two oysters and a few chopped chives
for garnish.
2. Place the remaining oysters and sour cream
into a blender or food processor and process for a
few seconds until smooth. Turn into a bowl and
stir in the chives. Season well with freshly ground
black pepper. Cover and chill.
3. Transfer the dip to a serving dish and garnish
with the reserved oysters. Sprinkle with the
chives. Serve with melba toast.

Avocado and Tuna Dip

MAKES ABOUT 1½ CUPS

1 medium ripe avocado
2 Tbsp lemon juice
3½ oz canned tuna in water or oil, well drained
½ cup mayonnaise
2 to 3 drops Worcester sauce
½ tsp English mustard
Freshly ground black pepper
Sprigs of flat-leaf parsley and strips of lemon rind
Cheese straws, strips of zucchini, carrot, green beans

1. Using a sharp knife, halve the avocado
lengthwise. Carefully twist the two halves in
opposing directions to separate the avocado.
Remove the pit and skin.
2. Cut the avocado flesh into chunks and place in
a bowl with the lemon juice. Using a fork, mash
the avocado into a pulp.
3. Flake the tuna into the avocado mixture. Add
the mayonnaise, Worcester sauce, and mustard,
mixing thoroughly. Season to taste with freshly
ground black pepper. Cover and chill.
4. Transfer the dip to a serving bowl, garnish with
sprigs of parsley and lemon rind. Serve with
cheese straws, strips of zucchini and carrot, and
blanched and cooled fine green beans.

Taramasalata

MAKES ABOUT 1½ CUPS

If possible use fresh smoked cod roe (fish eggs) or smoked soft roe – for this you may have to find a specialty fish merchant. If fresh cod roe is hard to find, then use "tamara" (pale orange carp roe) or red (whitefish) caviar.

7 oz fresh smoked cod roe
1 slice of white bread, crust removed
1 garlic clove, crushed
⅔ cup olive oil
Juice of ½ lemon
Freshly ground black pepper
Sprig of fresh parsley and lemon slices
Strips of warm pita bread

1. Place the roe in a bowl. Hold the bread under cold running water to wet it. Squeeze the excess water from the bread, then add it to the roe, along with the garlic. Mix thoroughly.
2. Add the olive oil *very gradually*, to the roe mixture, beating in each small addition thoroughly. It is important not to rush this stage or else the mixture will separate and curdle. The mixture should be smooth, pink, and creamy looking.
3. Stir in the lemon juice and season well with freshly ground black pepper. Cover and chill.
4. Spoon the taramasalata into a serving dish, garnish with the parsley and lemon slices. Serve with strips of warm pita bread.

Bagna Cauda

MAKES ABOUT 1¼ CUPS

If possible, keep this dip warm in a heatproof dish on a tabletop warmer or over a nightlight, while you and your friends dip into it with a selection of raw vegetables and bread.

2 oz canned anchovy fillets, drained
3 garlic cloves
4 Tbsp olive oil
4 Tbsp butter
⅔ cup heavy cream
Freshly ground black pepper
Strips of fennel, celery, and carrots, and cubed, crusty bread

1. Finely chop the anchovy fillets and crush the cloves of garlic.
2. Heat the olive oil and butter together and gently sauté the garlic for one minute. Add the anchovies and simmer over a low heat for ten minutes.
3. Remove from the heat and allow to cool slightly before pouring in the cream, mixing thoroughly. Return the pan to the heat and heat through gently. Season well with freshly ground black pepper. Serve the dip warm with strips of fennel, celery, carrot, and cubes of crusty bread.

Shrimp Cocktail Dip

MAKES ABOUT 1¼ CUPS

Use a selection of small crisp lettuce leaves to scoop up this dip.

6 oz cooked shelled shrimp (thawed, if frozen)
⅔ cup mayonnaise
1 tsp tomato paste
1 tsp white wine vinegar
3 to 5 drops hot chili sauce
1 small lemon
Freshly ground black pepper
Small crisp lettuce leaves, celery, cucumber strips, and melba toast

1. Drain any excess liquid from the shrimp. Chop them finely.
2. In a bowl, combine the mayonnaise, tomato purée, vinegar, and as many drops of hot sauce to suit your own taste. I usually find three to five drops give a nice piquancy without being overpowering.
3. Cut the lemon in half, reserving one half for garnish. Finely grate the rind, squeeze the juice from the other lemon half, and stir into the dip.
4. Mix the chopped shrimp into the mayonnaise mixture and season to taste with freshly ground black pepper. Cover and chill.
5. Spoon the dip into a serving dish and garnish with slices of lemon. Serve with a selection of individual crisp lettuce leaves, celery, cucumber strips, and melba toast.

Crab Dip

MAKES ABOUT 1½ CUPS

If you prefer a smoother-textured crab dip, you can purée everything together in a blender or food processor, but I feel it then loses its crab-meat texture. To add to the seaside feel of this dip, serve it in several large cleaned crab shells, if you can find them.

6 oz canned white crab meat, drained
½ cup plain yogurt
1 Tbsp lemon juice
1 tsp white wine vinegar
2 Tbsp fresh parsley, chopped
Freshly ground black pepper
Sprigs of fresh parsley
Chips and salty snacks

1. Place the crab meat in a bowl and with the back of a fork mash it into a fine shredded consistency.
2. Stir in the yogurt, lemon juice, wine vinegar, and parsley. Season well with freshly ground black pepper to taste. Cover and chill.
3. Spoon the dip into a serving bowl and garnish with sprigs of parsley. Serve with a selection of chips and other salty snacks.

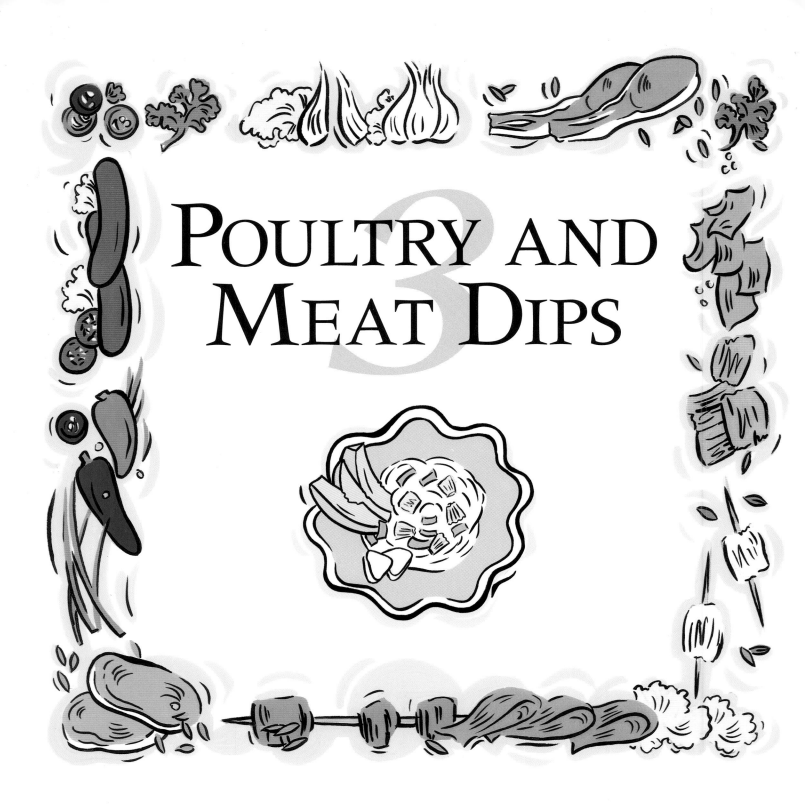

POULTRY AND MEAT DIPS

3

Peanut Satay Style Dip with Stir-Fried Pork Strips

MAKES ABOUT 1¼ CUPS

This Thai-based recipe has a rich peanut dip and is excellent served with marinated stir-fried strips of lean pork. Use fillet (tenderloin) of pork because it is a tender cut that can easily be stirfried. Serve both the dip and meat hot, straight from the pan. This will serve about six to eight people as a first course or four people as a main meal.

FOR THE DIP
1 oz shredded coconut
1 cup milk
1 tsp sunflower oil
1 inch piece of fresh ginger root, peeled and chopped fine
1 garlic clove, crushed
1 green chile, deseeded and chopped fine
⅔ cup crunchy peanut butter

FOR THE STIR-FRIED PORK STRIPS
1 lb fillet (tenderloin) of pork
3 Tbsp medium dry sherry
2 Tbsp dark soy sauce
2 tsp red wine vinegar
3 Tbsp sunflower oil, for frying

1. Cut the pork into thin bite-sized strips. Combine the sherry, soy sauce, and vinegar in a large bowl and add the pork, stirring well to ensure it is well coated in the marinade. Cover and chill until required for cooking.

2. Meanwhile, place the coconut and milk in a small, heavy-bottom saucepan and slowly bring to a boil, taking care not to scorch the milk. Remove from the heat and leave the coconut to infuse in the milk for at least thirty minutes.

3. **To make the Dip:** Strain the infused coconut and milk through a fine sieve over a bowl. Gently press the coconut with the back of a spoon to express as much coconut-flavored milk as possible. Discard the coconut.

4. Heat the sunflower oil in a saucepan and gently sauté the ginger, garlic, and chile for two to three minutes until tender, but not browned. Add the coconut-flavored milk and peanut butter. Heat gently, stirring continuously until the peanut butter has melted and combined with the other ingredients to make a smooth sauce. Simmer gently for five minutes. Remove from heat but keep warm until serving.

5. **To stir-fry the Pork Strips:** Heat the sunflower oil in a large frying pan or wok and cook the pork in several batches, stir-frying for about five to eight minutes, or until the meat is thoroughly cooked. The meat will turn a delicious brown color and the juices should be clear rather than bloody. Remove the cooked pork to a warmed serving dish and keep warm while cooking the remaining batches.

6. Spoon the peanut dip into a heatproof serving dish and serve with the stir-fried pork strips. If serving this as a main meal you may also wish to serve vegetable accompaniments such as strips of cucumber and bell peppers and trimmed scallions.

Quick Tangy Tomato Dip with Turkey Dipping Sticks

MAKES ABOUT 1 CUP

SERVES SIX AS A STARTER, FOUR AS A MAIN MEAL WITH ACCOMPANIMENTS

Bread-crumb and batter-coated nuggets or strips of meats and fish are readily available from most supermarkets, fresh or frozen, but sometimes it's great to have a go yourself and make your own. This quick and easy batter recipe can be applied to many of the other dips since the batter can coat fish, meat, poultry, and vegetables such as onion rings or zucchini slices. It is also used to coat apple rings (see the sweet Cinnamon and Raisin Yogurt Dip on page 57). Happy dipping!

FOR THE DIP
4 Tbsp ketchup
4 Tbsp pourable honey
1 Tbsp light brown sugar
1 Tbsp red wine vinegar
⅓ cup fresh orange juice
2–3 drops of hot sauce
1 tsp dry sherry

FOR THE TURKEY DIPPING STICKS

BATTER
MAKES ABOUT 1¼ CUPS

½ cup all-purpose flour
Salt and pepper
1 egg, beaten
¾ cup milk

TURKEY STICKS
1lb skinless and boneless turkey breast meat
¼ cup all-purpose flour, seasoned with salt and pepper
Vegetable oil, for deep frying

To accompany if serving as a main meal: French fries, raw strips of celery, cucumber, and zucchini

1. To make the Dip: Simply combine all the dip ingredients together in a bowl. Cover and chill.

2. To make the Batter: Sift the flour into a bowl and season with salt and pepper, making a well in the center. Combine the beaten egg with the milk and gradually blend into the flour, using a fork to make a smooth batter. This can be made well in advance, covered, and kept in the refrigerator until required.

3. To make the Turkey Sticks: Cut the turkey breast meat into even-sized pieces about two inches by one-quarter inch. Place the seasoned flour in a small, clean plastic bag and add about a quarter of the turkey strips at a time. Hold the bag at the top to seal and shake the turkey strips until evenly coated in the flour. Remove the coated turkey from the bag to a plate and repeat for the remaining turkey.

4. Heat the oil in a large heavy-bottom pan to 355°F. Dip the coated turkey strips a few at a time in the batter, allowing the excess batter to run from the meat. Fry in the oil for about eight to ten minutes, until golden and the turkey is thoroughly cooked through. Drain on paper towels and keep warm while frying the remaining batter-coated turkey in batches.

5. Serve the warm turkey strips with the dip, which can be served chilled or warm. If serving as a main meal, accompany the dip with French fries and strips of celery, cucumber, and zucchini.

Ham and Gruyère Dip

MAKES ABOUT 1½ CUPS

Gruyère cheese has a sweet flavor and delicious nutty aroma that complements the ham in this dip. Served in hollowed-out crusty bread rolls with strips of raw cucumber, celery, and carrot, this dip makes a filling lunchtime snack.

7 oz sour cream
½ tsp Dijon mustard
3 oz cooked lean ham
3 oz Gruyère cheese
1 Tbsp fresh parsley, chopped
Freshly ground black pepper
Hollowed-out crusty bread rolls (optional)
Strips of cucumber, celery, and carrot

1. Place the sour cream and mustard in a bowl and mix thoroughly.

2. Finely dice the ham. Finely grate the Gruyère cheese. Add the ham and cheese to the sour cream and combine well. Stir in the parsley. Season well with freshly ground black pepper. Cover and chill.

3. Transfer the dip to a serving bowl or hollowed-out crusty bread rolls. Serve with strips of cucumber, celery, and carrot.

Smoky Bacon and Cream Cheese Dip

MAKES ABOUT 1¼ CUPS

For best effect chill this dip for at least two hours so that the smoky bacon flavor matures in the cream cheese.

6 oz smoked bacon slices, cooked until crispy and cooled
7 oz cream cheese
¼ cup plain yogurt
2 Tbsp milk
Freshly ground black pepper
1 Tbsp fresh chives, chopped
Breadsticks, a selection of crackers, and strips of celery

1. Blend the cream cheese, yogurt, and milk together in a bowl.

2. Crumble the cooked bacon into little pieces. Reserve one tablespoon for garnish and stir the remaining bacon into the cream cheese mixture. Season well with freshly ground black pepper. Cover and chill.

3. Spoon the dip into a serving dish and sprinkle with the chopped chives and reserved crumbled bacon. Serve with breadsticks, a selection of crackers, and strips of celery.

Smoked Ham and Pineapple Dip

MAKES ABOUT 1½ CUPS

This dip needs to be chilled to allow the smoked ham flavor to mingle with the cream cheese. Serve the dip with bite-sized wedges of peeled mango, papaya, and melon for a tropical flourish.

7 oz cream cheese
4 oz cooked smoked ham, sliced
1 cup canned pineapple pieces in natural juice, drained
Freshly ground black pepper
Sprig of fresh parsley
Small wedges of peeled mango, papaya, and melon

1. Place the cream cheese, half of the smoked ham, and half of the pineapple pieces into a blender or food processor and process for a few seconds until smooth. Transfer the mixture to a bowl.

2. Finely chop the remaining ham and pineapple pieces and lightly stir into the cheese mixture to add color and texture. Season well with freshly ground black pepper. Cover and chill.

3. Spoon the dip into a serving dish and garnish with a sprig of fresh parsley. Serve with peeled, bite-sized wedges of mango, papaya, and melon.

Beef and Creamed Horseradish Dip

MAKES ABOUT 1½ CUPS

This dip makes an excellent casual lunch and is great to eat with fresh French fries while watching television.

1 cup sour cream
4 oz cooked lean beef, chopped
2 tsp creamed horseradish sauce
Freshly ground black pepper
Sprigs of fresh parsley
Wedges of tomato, crisp lettuce leaves, and French fries

1. Place the sour cream, cooked beef, and horseradish sauce in a blender or food processor and process for a few seconds until smooth. Transfer to a bowl and season well with freshly ground black pepper. Cover and chill.
2. Spoon the dip into a serving dish or individual ramekins and garnish with sprigs of fresh parsley. Serve with wedges of tomato, crisp lettuce leaves, and plenty of hot French fries for a hearty feast.

Roasted Peanut and Ham Dip

MAKES ABOUT 1½ CUPS

⅔ cup sour cream
4 oz smoked lean ham slices, chopped
4 oz roasted peanuts, coarsely chopped
5 to 6 drops Worcester sauce
Pinch of cayenne pepper
Breadsticks, chips, crackers, a selection of raw strips of vegetables such as celery, cucumber, carrot, and wedges of tomato

1. Place the sour cream and ham in a blender or food processor and process for a few seconds until smooth and well combined. Turn the ham mixture into a bowl.
2. Add the peanuts, reserving a tablespoonful for garnish.
3. Season the dip with Worcester sauce and cayenne pepper. Cover and chill.
4. Transfer the dip to a serving bowl and garnish with the reserved peanuts. Serve with breadsticks, chips, and crackers, plus raw strips of celery, cucumber, and carrot, and wedges of tomato.

Chorizo Sausage and Tomato Dip

MAKES ABOUT 1½ CUPS

Chorizo sausages are Spanish cooked sausages with a spicy, garlic flavor. If you cannot find Chorizo sausages, use any cooked garlic sausage. Serve with chunks of crusty bread or garlic bread to scoop out the spicy sausage.

1 Tbsp olive oil
2 Tbsp onion, chopped fine
5 oz Chorizo sausages, chopped fine
14 oz canned chopped tomatoes in tomato juice, drained
1 tsp tomato paste
1 tsp fresh thyme leaves, stalks removed
Chunks of crusty bread or garlic bread

1. Heat the oil in a saucepan and add the onion and Chorizo sausages. Sauté for five minutes over moderate heat, until the onion is tender.
2. Add the tomatoes, tomato paste and thyme and simmer for ten minutes. Turn into a heatproof serving dish and serve warm with crusty bread or garlic bread.

Chicken Liver and Mushroom Dip

MAKES ABOUT 1½ CUPS

This has the richness of a pâté but the moister texture of a dip. It will serve six to eight as a starter, four to six as a snack lunch.

4 Tbsp olive oil
1 medium onion, chopped
1 garlic clove, crushed
7 oz open mushrooms, chopped fine
8 oz chicken livers, cut into even-sized pieces
1 Tbsp brandy (optional)
Salt and freshly ground black pepper
2 Tbsp fresh parsley, chopped
Melba toast, ryebread, and crackers

1. Heat the olive oil in a saucepan. Sauté the onion and garlic for about four to five minutes over moderate heat, until tender, but not browned. Stir occasionally.
2. Add the mushrooms to the onion mixture. Cook over moderate heat for about five minutes until the mushrooms have cooked down.
3. Add the chicken livers to the pan. Simmer for about five minutes, stirring occasionally, until the chicken livers are cooked. Test by cutting a piece in half: the liver should be gray in color with no blood present. As soon as the liver is cooked, remove from the heat, transfer to a bowl, and allow to cool for ten minutes.
4. Place the cooled chicken liver mixture into a blender or food processor, along with the brandy, if desired. Process until smooth. Season to taste with salt and black pepper. Cover and chill.
5. Spoon the dip into a serving dish and sprinkle with the chopped parsley. Serve with melba toast, ryebread, and crackers.

Chicken and Almond Dip

MAKES ABOUT 1¾ CUPS

The celery and toasted almonds add a surprising crunch to this creamy chicken dip.

2 oz chopped blanched almonds
5 oz cooked boneless and skinless chicken breast
1 cup whole plain yogurt
2 celery sticks, chopped fine
Freshly ground black pepper
Cubed bagels or crusty bread, strips of cucumber, carrot, bell peppers, and zucchini

1. Sprinkle the chopped almonds in a single layer on a sheet of aluminum foil. Place under a hot pre-heated broiler and toast until a pale golden brown, turning occasionally, so they brown evenly. Take care that they don't brown too suddenly. Remove from the broiler and allow to cool completely.
2. Coarsely chop the chicken and place in a blender or food processor along with the yogurt. Process for a few seconds until smooth. Turn the chicken mixture into a bowl.
3. Reserve a tablespoon of chopped celery and toasted almonds for a garnish and mix the remaining celery and nuts into the chicken mixture. Season well with freshly ground black pepper. Cover and chill.
4. To serve, spoon the dip into a serving bowl and sprinkle with the reserved chopped celery and toasted almonds. Serve with cubed pieces of bagel or crusty bread and strips of cucumber, carrot, bell peppers, and zucchini.

VEGETABLE DIPS

Tzatziki

MAKES ABOUT 1¼ CUPS

With this traditional, chilled Greek dip, cut small firm zucchini into long thin strips, coat in seasoned flour, and pan-fry in olive oil until golden – serve warm.

½ cucumber (7 inches)
⅔ cup whole plain yogurt
1 garlic clove, crushed
1 tsp white wine vinegar
3 Tbsp fresh mint, chopped
1 Tbsp olive oil
Freshly ground black pepper
Cucumber slices and mint sprigs
Pan-fried strips of zucchini

1. Peel the cucumber, cut in half lengthwise. Using a teaspoon, scoop out the seeds. Coarsely grate the cucumber flesh into a bowl. Drain any excess liquid collected in the bowl from the grated cucumber.
2. Add the yogurt, garlic, vinegar, mint, and olive oil to the cucumber and mix well. Season well with freshly ground black pepper. Cover and chill.
3. Transfer the tzatziki to a serving dish and garnish with cucumber slices and sprigs of mint. Serve with warm, pan-fried zucchini strips.

Watercress and Yogurt Dip

MAKES ABOUT 1¼ CUPS

4 oz fresh watercress, washed
⅔ cup plain lowfat yogurt
Freshly ground black pepper
Crisp small lettuce leaves, celery, and carrot strips; cooked salmon or white fish pieces, crumb- or batter-coated

1. Reserve a few watercress sprigs for a garnish. Make sure the watercress is well drained, then place in a blender or food processor with the yogurt and process for a few seconds until well combined. Season with freshly ground black pepper.
2. Pour the dip into a serving dish and garnish with the watercress sprigs. Serve with small, crisp lettuce leaves with which to scoop up the dip and strips of celery and carrot. Salmon strips coated in bread crumbs or batter and fried or baked are wonderful served warm with this dip, although any white fish such as cod, hoki, or haddock served in this way are all extremely good accompaniments.

Black Olive Dip

MAKES ABOUT 1½ CUPS

14 oz canned pitted black olives in brine, drained
2 garlic cloves, crushed
1 Tbsp tomato paste
1 Tbsp olive oil
1 beefsteak tomato, skinned, deseeded, and chopped fine
Freshly ground black pepper
Fresh basil leaves
Thin wedges of olive bread or Ciabatta

1. Place the drained olives, garlic, tomato paste, and olive oil in a blender or food processor and process for a few seconds so that the olives retain some texture and are not completely smooth.
2. Transfer the mixture to a bowl and stir in the chopped tomato. Season well with freshly ground black pepper. Cover and chill.
3. Transfer the dip to a serving bowl and garnish with fresh basil leaves. Serve with wedges of olive bread or Ciabatta.

Scarlet Delight Dip

MAKES ABOUT 1½ CUPS

This dip has a stunning appearance but is not for the faint-hearted. It tastes wonderful on any occasion but its beet-red color makes it particularly well suited for a Halloween party!

1 orange
7 oz cooked beets
⅔ cup sour cream
Freshly ground black pepper
Strips of fennel, celery, zucchini, and cucumber

1. Make the orange rind garnish: With a zester or vegetable peeler, remove a few strips of rind from the orange. If using a vegetable peeler, the pieces of rind will need to be cut into very fine strips with a sharp knife.

2. Roughly chop the cooked beets and place in a blender or food processor with the juice from the orange and blend until smooth.

3. Tip the beet mixture into a bowl and add three-quarters of the sour cream, mixing thoroughly. Season to taste with freshly ground black pepper. Cover and chill.

4. To serve, turn the beet dip into a serving dish and lightly swirl in the remaining sour cream. Garnish with the orange rind. Serve with strips of fennel, celery, zucchini, and cucumber.

Scallion Dip

MAKES ABOUT 1¼ CUPS

¼ cup scallions, chopped fine
⅔ cup sour cream
¼ cup plain yogurt
1 tsp paprika
Freshly ground black pepper
Crisp lettuce leaves, strips of zucchini and bell peppers,
and potato chips

1. Reserve one tablespoon of the chopped scallions for garnish. Place the remaining scallions, sour cream, yogurt, and paprika in a bowl and mix thoroughly. Season to taste with freshly ground black pepper. Cover and chill.
2. Spoon the dip into a serving bowl and sprinkle with the reserved chopped scallions. Serve with crisp lettuce leaves, strips of zucchini and bell peppers, and potato chips.

Sweet and Sour Dip with Chinese Vegetables

MAKES ABOUT 1¾ CUPS

1 Tbsp peanut oil
2 scallions, chopped
1 small yellow bell pepper, deseeded and chopped fine
1 small green bell pepper, deseeded and chopped fine
14 oz canned chopped tomatoes in tomato juice, drained
2 Tbsp red wine vinegar
1 Tbsp dry sherry
1 Tbsp light brown sugar
Strips of celery, cucumber, carrot, yellow and red bell
peppers, canned water chestnuts (drained), baby sweetcorn
and snow peas (blanched and chilled), and shrimp crackers

1. Heat the oil in a saucepan and fry the scallions and peppers for about five minutes over a moderate heat until tender but not browned, stirring occasionally.
2. Add the tomatoes, vinegar, sherry, and brown sugar. Simmer for five minutes, remove from the heat, and allow to cool. Cover and chill.
3. Transfer the dip to a serving bowl and serve with strips of raw vegetables, drained canned water chestnuts, and briefly blanched baby sweetcorn and snow peas. Shrimp crackers are also ideal dipping accompaniments.

Radish Dip

MAKES ABOUT 1½ CUPS

This pretty pink dip has a refreshingly light flavor.

5 oz radishes, leaves removed
½ cup mayonnaise
⅔ cup sour cream
2 tsp lemon juice
Freshly ground black pepper
Crisp lettuce leaves, strips of cucumber and celery, cooked
peeled jumbo shrimp

1. Reserve one radish for garnish. Place the remaining radishes in a food processor with a fine grater disk or finely grate the radishes by hand. Drain any excess liquid.
2. Turn the grated radish into a bowl and stir in the mayonnaise, sour cream, and lemon juice. Season well with freshly ground black pepper. Cover and chill.
3. Turn the dip into a serving bowl and garnish with slices cut from the reserved radish. Serve with crisp lettuce leaves, strips of cucumber and celery, and cooked, peeled jumbo shrimp.

Tomato and Basil Dip

MAKES ABOUT 1½ CUPS

This dip makes a colorful first course. It can be prepared in advance and served in the hollowed-out tomatoes.

4 beefsteak tomatoes
1 small onion, chopped
6 Tbsp fresh basil, chopped
Freshly ground black pepper
Fresh basil leaves
Breadsticks, strips of cucumber, celery, and zucchini

1. To hollow out the tomatoes, first cut the top off of the tomatoes in a thin slice. With a sharp knife, cut around the inner flesh of each of the tomatoes and scoop out the central flesh and seeds with a spoon. Place the four hollowed-out tomatoes upside down on a plate to allow excess juice to drain out.

2. Discard the tomato seeds and finely dice the tomato flesh. Place the chopped tomato in a nonmetallic sieve and press out any excess juice.

3. Place half of the chopped tomato and all of the chopped onion in a blender or food processor and process for a few seconds until smooth. Transfer the mixture to a bowl.

4. Stir in the remaining chopped tomato and chopped fresh basil. Season well with freshly ground black pepper. Divide the dip mixture evenly among the four hollowed-out tomatoes. Cover and chill.

5. Garnish with fresh basil leaves just before serving. Serve with breadsticks and strips of cucumber, celery, and zucchini.

Sundried Tomato Stunner Dip

MAKES ABOUT 1½ CUPS

Sundried tomatoes give this dip a really rich flavor, so serve it with strips of bell peppers and slices of warm garlic bread.

14 oz canned tomatoes in tomato juice, drained and chopped
1 small yellow bell pepper
3 oz sundried tomatoes in olive oil, drained
1 Tbsp fresh basil, chopped
1 Tbsp fresh oregano, chopped
Freshly ground black pepper
Fresh basil and oregano leaves
Strips of yellow, orange, red, and green bell pepper, warm garlic bread, sliced

1. Cut the yellow pepper in half lengthwise and remove the stalk and seeds. Roughly chop one-half of the pepper and place in a blender or food processor along with the tomatoes and sundried tomatoes. Process for a few seconds until smooth.

2. Transfer the tomato mixture to a bowl and stir in the chopped basil and oregano. Finely dice the remaining half of the yellow pepper and add to the dip. Season with freshly ground black pepper. Cover and chill.

3. Spoon the dip into a serving dish and garnish with basil and oregano leaves. Serve with strips of colorful peppers and slices of warm garlic bread.

Puréed Vegetable and Pumpkin Seed Dip

MAKES ABOUT 1½ CUPS

This dip can be served hot or cold.

1 Tbsp olive oil
1 medium onion, chopped fine
1 garlic clove, crushed (optional)
1 small yellow-fleshed squash (you need about ¾ cup chopped flesh)
1 medium red bell pepper
1 tsp fresh thyme leaves
¼ cup vegetable stock OR cold water
3 Tbsp pumpkin seeds
Small wedges of a selection of breads, e.g. Ciabatta, tomato bread, olive bread, and pumpernickel

1. Heat the olive oil in a saucepan, add the onion and garlic, and sauté gently for five minutes, until tender but not browned. Stir occasionally.

2. Meanwhile, cut the squash in half and scoop out the seeds. Cut the halves into wedges and using a sharp vegetable peeler or knife, remove the squash skin. Cut the squash flesh into one-inch pieces. Cut the red pepper in half lengthwise, remove the seeds and dice the pepper flesh.

3. Add the squash, red pepper, and thyme to the onion and fry for two minutes. Add the vegetable stock OR cold water, bring to a boil, cover, and simmer for fifteen minutes, or until the squash is just tender. Stir occasionally. Allow to cool for at least ten minutes before puréeing.

4. Lightly toast the pumpkin seeds under a hot preheated broiler or grill – this only takes a minute or two, so don't leave them unattended! The pumpkin seeds begin to make a popping sound when they are ready. Remove from the broiler and leave to cool.

5. Place the vegetable mixture and all but one tablespoon of the pumpkin seeds into a blender or food processor. Process for a few seconds on a pulse setting if possible, so that the dip retains some texture rather than being completely smooth.

6. Transfer to a serving dish and serve warm or allow to cool, then cover and chill in the refrigerator. Sprinkle with the remaining toasted pumpkin seeds just before serving. Serve with a selection of flavored breads such as Ciabatta, tomato, olive, and pumpernickel cut into suitable dipping-sized wedges.

Quick and Easy BBQ Dip

MAKES ABOUT 1½ CUPS

Serve this dip warm or cold and don't just wait for the barbecue season – it tastes as good with broiled chicken drumsticks, spare ribs, and sausages as it does with broiled yellow and green bell pepper quarters.

1 Tbsp olive oil
1 medium onion, chopped fine
14 oz canned tomatoes in tomato juice, chopped
2 Tbsp brown sauce
2 tsp soft brown sugar
Hot sauce
Barbecued or well broiled chicken drumsticks, spare ribs, sausages, and yellow and green bell peppers

1. Heat the olive oil in a saucepan and fry the chopped onion for about five minutes, until tender and lightly browned.
2. Meanwhile, drain the chopped tomatoes, reserving the juice.
3. Add the drained tomatoes, brown sauce, and sugar to the frying onions. Add a few drops of hot sauce to taste. Simmer the dip for ten minutes, adding a little of the reserved tomato juice if the dip becomes too thick.
4. Serve the dip warm or cool – cover and chill in the refrigerator until required. Serve with barbecued or well broiled chicken drumsticks, spare ribs, sausages, and quarters of yellow and green bell peppers that have been broiled or grilled until slightly charred.

Guacamole

MAKES ABOUT 1¾ CUPS

2 medium ripe avocados
3 Tbsp lemon juice
1 garlic clove, crushed
2 tomatoes, chopped, skinned, and deseeded
2 scallions, chopped fine
1 green chile, deseeded and chopped fine
1 Tbsp fresh coriander, chopped fine
Freshly ground black pepper
Tortilla chips and strips of bell pepper

1. Cut the avocados in half lengthwise. Twist the halves in opposite directions to separate the two halves. Remove the central pit and peel away the skin. Chop the avocado flesh into chunks.
2. Place the avocado into a mixing bowl along with the lemon juice and garlic and mash until fairly smooth with the back of a fork.
3. In a small bowl, mix together the tomato, scallions, chile, and coriander. Reserve one tablespoon of the mix for garnish and add the rest to the avocado mixture. Combine thoroughly. Season to taste with freshly ground black pepper.
4. Place the guacamole in a serving dish and garnish with the reserved tomato, scallions, chile, and coriander. Cover and chill.
5. Serve the guacamole dip with tortilla chips and colorful strips of bell pepper. For those who like it hot, raw chiles can also be dipped!

Eggplant and Pepper Dip

MAKES ABOUT 1½ CUPS

Broiling vegetables adds a delicious Mediterranean flavor to this dip. The eggplant does not necessarily have to be peeled.

1 eggplant (weighing about 12 oz)
1 medium onion
1 medium green bell pepper
1 garlic clove (optional)
¼ cup olive oil
Freshly ground black pepper
Slices of warm garlic bread

1. Preheat the broiler. Cut the eggplant into one-half-inch rounds, discarding the top stalk. Peel the onion and also cut into one-half-inch slices. Halve the green pepper lengthwise.
2. Place the eggplant, onion, pepper halves (skin side facing up), and garlic clove onto a heatproof tray, brush with olive oil, and season with freshly ground black pepper. Place the vegetables under the broiler and cook for about fifteen minutes, until the eggplant slices turn a golden brown and the onion rings caramelize. When one side is browned, turn them over, brush with olive oil, season, and cook until browned. The green pepper should be cooked until the skin blackens and the garlic clove should soften and the skin char.
3. When the vegetables are cooked, remove them to a dish and allow to cool completely.
4. Remove the blackened skin from the cooled green pepper. Remove the stalk and seeds and chop the cooked pepper flesh.
5. Place all of the cooked vegetables in a blender or food processor and process for a few seconds until smooth. Spoon into a bowl, cover, and chill.
6. Serve with slices of warm crusty garlic bread.

Smooth Chile Tomato Dip

MAKES ABOUT 1¾ CUPS

This cheerful and fiery red dip can be served warm or chilled. If served warm with plenty of dipping accompaniments, it makes a substantial main meal.

2 Tbsp olive oil
1 medium onion, chopped fine
3 red chiles, deseeded and chopped fine
2 garlic cloves, crushed
14 oz canned plum tomatoes in tomato juice
1 tsp red wine vinegar
2 tsp fine granulated sugar
Freshly ground black pepper
Cooked, peeled jumbo shrimp, deep-fried batter-coated vegetables, e.g. onion rings, cauliflower and broccoli florets; strips of pita bread and bell peppers

1. Heat the olive oil in a saucepan, add the onion, chiles, and garlic. Sauté gently for five minutes, stirring occasionally.
2. Add the canned tomatoes and their juice, the vinegar, and sugar to the fried onion mixture. Break the tomatoes up with a wooden spoon. Bring to a boil, cover, and simmer for twenty-five minutes.
3. Allow to cool for ten minutes before processing in a blender or food processor until smooth. Season to taste with freshly ground black pepper. Turn into a heatproof serving dish if serving warm, or allow to cool completely then chill in the refrigerator, if serving cold. Serve with peeled, cooked jumbo shrimp, deep-fried batter-coated vegetables, and strips of pita bread and colorful bell peppers.

Sesame and Red Pepper Dip

MAKES ABOUT 1¼ CUPS

A distinctive taste of the Orient adds a characteristic note to this sesame dip.

1 Tbsp sunflower oil
½ tsp sesame oil
1 inch cube fresh root ginger, peeled and chopped fine
1 garlic clove, crushed
14 oz red bell peppers, deseeded and diced fine
⅔ cup chicken OR vegetable stock
2 Tbsp medium dry sherry
1 Tbsp sesame seeds
Rice and shrimp crackers; blanched and cooled snow peas and baby sweetcorn; strips of celery and cucumber

1. Heat the sunflower and sesame oil in a saucepan, add the ginger and garlic, and sauté gently for two to three minutes until softened but not browned. Add the peppers and sauté for another five minutes.

2. Add the stock and sherry, bring to a boil, and simmer for fifteen minutes. Leave to cool.

3. Meanwhile, place the sesame seeds in a single layer on a sheet of aluminum foil on a baking tray. Place under a moderately hot broiler for about two to three minutes, until lightly browned. Turn them occasionally so they toast evenly and take care that they do not brown suddenly. Remove from the broiler and leave to cool.

4. Place the cooled red pepper mixture into a blender or food processor, retaining some of the cooking liquid in the saucepan. Add half of the toasted sesame seeds and process for a few seconds until the mixture is smooth – don't worry if some of the sesame seeds remain unblended. Check the consistency of the red pepper mixture: If it is too firm for a dip, add a little of the reserved cooking liquid until you obtain a fairly thin consistency.

5. Transfer the dip to a serving dish and chill until required.

6. Just before serving, sprinkle with the remaining toasted sesame seeds. Serve with rice and shrimp crackers, blanched and cooled snow peas and baby sweetcorn, and strips of celery and cucumber.

Asparagus Cream Dip

MAKES ABOUT 1¼ CUPS

Use fresh young asparagus for this dip. It's very easy to make and tastes divine.

9 oz fresh young asparagus
½ cup heavy cream
Freshly ground black pepper
Trimmed fine green beans, endive, and young asparagus for dipping

1. Cut the asparagus for the dip into one-inch pieces. Place all the asparagus in a small saucepan with ⅔ cup cold water, bring to a boil, cover, and simmer for about eight to ten minutes, until just tender. Drain and refresh under cold running water. Drain well and leave to cool completely. Reserve the spears for dipping.

2. Place the cold asparagus pieces in a blender or food processor and blend for a few seconds until smooth. If necessary add one to two tablespoons of cream to help process the asparagus.

3. Lightly whip the remaining cream in a bowl, then stir in the asparagus. Season well with freshly ground black pepper. Cover and chill.

4. Spoon the dip into a serving bowl. Serve with the asparagus spears and fine, chilled green beans, plus endive leaves. If serving this dip as a first course when entertaining, spoon into individual ramekin dishes.

Artichoke Heart Dip

MAKES ABOUT 1½ CUPS

14 oz canned artichoke hearts, well drained
7 oz cream cheese
¼ cup heavy cream
Freshly ground black pepper
Broiled or grilled vegetables, e.g. strips of red and yellow
bell pepper, zucchini, and eggplant

1. Place the well-drained artichoke hearts, cream cheese, and cream in a blender or food processor and process for a few seconds until smooth and well combined. Turn the dip into a bowl, season to taste, cover, and chill.

2. Spoon the dip into a serving dish. Serve with strips of red and yellow bell pepper, zucchini, and eggplant that have been brushed with olive oil, seasoned, and broiled until tender. Don't worry if some of the skins char slightly as this adds flavor.

Celery and Spinach Dip

MAKES ABOUT 1½ CUPS

Use young leaf spinach and cut it very finely so it will blend into the dip. The crisp celery adds a light crunch. Serve this fairly thick dip with a selection of cheese crackers.

7 oz cream cheese
¼ cup mayonnaise
3 Tbsp milk
1 garlic clove, crushed (optional)
2 celery stalks, chopped fine
2 oz young baby leaves of spinach
Freshly ground black pepper
Selection of small cheese crackers

1. Soften the cream cheese with the mayonnaise in a bowl. Blend in the milk and garlic, if using. Stir in the celery.

2. Wash the spinach and remove any coarse stalks. Drain well and pat dry with kitchen towels. Roll up small bunches of spinach leaves and cut into fine shreds with a sharp knife. Stir the shredded spinach into the dip. Season well with freshly ground black pepper. Cover and chill.

3. Turn the dip into a serving bowl. Serve with a selection of small cheese crackers.

Tomato and Onion Sambal

MAKES ABOUT 1¾ CUPS

2 large tomatoes, deseeded and diced fine
1 medium onion, chopped fine
2 Tbsp lemon juice
½ tsp cumin seeds
A good pinch cayenne pepper
Strips of pita bread and crusty bread

1. Place the chopped tomato, onion, lemon juice, cumin seeds, and cayenne into a bowl and mix thoroughly. Cover and chill.

2. Serve the sambal with traditional Indian foods such as strips of pita bread cut wide enough to scoop up the chopped pieces of vegetables. Crusty bread is also an ideal accompaniment.

Tomato and Chile Salsa

MAKES ABOUT 1¾ CUPS

2 large tomatoes, deseeded and diced fine
1 medium onion, chopped fine
3 green chiles, deseeded and chopped fine
2 Tbsp fresh coriander, chopped
Freshly ground black pepper
Fresh coriander leaves
Wide strips of red, yellow, green, and orange bell peppers,
and tortilla chips

1. Place the tomato, onion, chiles, and coriander in a bowl and mix thoroughly. Season well with freshly ground black pepper. Cover and chill.

2. Transfer the salsa to a serving dish and garnish with coriander leaves. Serve pieces of different colored bell peppers, cut wide enough to scoop up the salsa, and tortilla chips as accompaniments.

Butternut Squash Dip

MAKES ABOUT 1¼ CUPS

Butternut squash and nutmeg have a lovely sweet and warming quality as a dip. The dip can be served warm or chilled, but I prefer it served warm with sweet potatoes cooked with their skins on, cut into wedges, and fried or oven roasted. A true winter comfort food.

1 butternut squash, weighing about 1½ lb
½ tsp nutmeg, freshly grated, plus a little to serve
¼ cup heavy cream
Freshly ground black pepper
Fried or oven roasted sweet potato wedges with their skins on

1. Cut the butternut squash in half lengthwise. Scoop out the seeds. Using a sharp knife or vegetable peeler carefully remove the skin. Cut the flesh into one-inch chunks.
2. Place the cubes of squash into a saucepan with ⅔ cup cold water and ½ tsp freshly grated nutmeg. Bring to a boil, cover, and simmer for about ten minutes, until just tender. Stir and turn the pieces of squash occasionally, so they cook evenly in the small quantity of water used. Take care not to overcook the squash.
3. Drain the cooked squash well and allow to cool slightly, then purée for a few seconds in a food processor or blender until smooth.
4. Stir in the cream, season, and serve immediately or allow to cool completely, cover, and chill in the refrigerator.
5. Just before serving the dip, grate a little more nutmeg on top and serve with fried or baked sweet potato wedges.

Mushroom and Pine Nut Dip

MAKES ABOUT 1¼ CUPS

Use large, flat-open mushrooms because they have a stronger mushroom flavor than the small button variety.

4 Tbsp olive oil
9 oz large open mushrooms, chopped fine
8 oz canned tomatoes in tomato juice, drained and chopped
2 oz pine nuts
Freshly ground black pepper
1 Tbsp fresh parsley, chopped
A selection of crackers and strips of crusty bread

1. Heat the oil in a saucepan and sauté the chopped mushrooms. Cook for about ten minutes over a moderate heat so that the juices released from the mushrooms evaporate and only the olive oil and concentrated cooked mushrooms are left in the pan. Stir occasionally. Leave to cool.
2. Meanwhile, place the pine nuts in a single layer on a heatproof baking sheet and place under a hot, preheated broiler or grill. Broil for one to two minutes, until the pine nuts turn a pale golden color, turn them occasionally so they toast evenly. Take care that the pine nuts don't suddenly turn brown and burn. Remove from the heat and allow to cool.
3. Place the mushrooms and any olive oil from the pan, the tomatoes, and all but one tablespoon of pine nuts in a blender or food processor. Process for a few seconds until smooth. Transfer to a bowl and season to taste. Cover and chill.
4. Spoon the dip into a serving bowl and sprinkle with the reserved pine nuts and chopped parsley. Serve with a selection of crackers and strips of crusty bread.

Creamy Corn Dip

MAKES ABOUT 1½ CUPS

4 oz sweetcorn kernels (canned or frozen)
⅔ cup heavy cream
1 oz Parmesan, freshly grated
2 Tbsp mayonnaise
1 Tbsp fresh chives, chopped
Freshly ground black pepper
Cheese straws, cubed bagels, and strips of cucumber,
carrot, and celery

1. If using canned sweetcorn, drain it well. Alternatively, if using frozen sweetcorn, cook in boiling water, drain, and cool completely. Reserve a tablespoon of sweetcorn for garnish.
2. Lightly whip the cream and stir in the remaining sweetcorn, Parmesan, mayonnaise, and chives. Season to taste with freshly ground black pepper. Cover and chill.
3. Spoon the dip into a serving bowl and sprinkle with the reserved sweetcorn. Serve with cheese straws, cubed bagels, and strips of cucumber, carrot, and celery.

Cucumber and Lime Raita

MAKES ABOUT 1¼ CUPS

½ cucumber (7 inches)
⅔ cup plain yogurt
1 garlic clove, crushed
2 Tbsp celery leaves, chopped fine
1 lime, juice and rind, grated fine
Freshly ground black pepper
Celery leaves
Strips of warm pita bread, cubes of crusty bread, and
strips of cucumber and celery

1. Peel the cucumber, cut in half lengthwise. Using a teaspoon, scoop out the seeds. Coarsely grate the cucumber flesh into a bowl. Drain any excess liquid collected in the bowl from the grated cucumber.
2. Add the yogurt, garlic, celery leaves, lime juice and rind, mixing thoroughly. Season to taste with freshly ground black pepper. Cover and chill.
3. Transfer the raita to a serving dish and garnish with celery leaves. Serve with strips of warm pita bread, cubes of crusty bread, and strips of cucumber and celery.

Tapenade

MAKES ABOUT 1¼ CUPS

7 oz pitted black olives
1 Tbsp capers, drained
1 garlic clove, crushed
2 tsp Dijon mustard
2 tsp lemon juice
½ cup olive oil
Freshly ground black pepper
Toasted crusty bread slices and olive bread

1. Reserve a couple of olives for a garnish. Place the remaining olives, capers, garlic, mustard, and lemon juice in a blender or food processor and process for a few seconds until smooth.
2. Add the olive oil *gradually* through the hole in the lid while the blender or processor is running. The oil must be added gradually so that the mixture is well emulsified and smooth. Turn the tapenade into a bowl and season with freshly ground black pepper. Cover and chill for at least two hours to let the flavors develop.
3. Spoon the tapenade into a serving bowl and garnish with reserved olives. Serve with toasted crusty bread and olive bread if available.

BEAN AND LENTIL 5 DIPS

Hummus

MAKES ABOUT 1½ CUPS

Although this dip can be processed until smooth, I prefer to leave it quite chunky so that the chickpeas give it some texture and bite. Enjoy the dip as a light lunch or at parties.

1 Tbsp sesame seeds
15 oz canned chickpeas, drained
3 garlic cloves, crushed
3 Tbsp olive oil
3 Tbsp lemon juice
Freshly ground black pepper
Sprig of fresh parsley
Strips of warm pita bread, and bell peppers, celery, and cucumber

1. Place the sesame seeds in a single layer on a piece of aluminum foil on a baking tray. Place under a moderately hot preheated broiler for about two to three minutes, until they are lightly toasted. Take care that they don't burn. Stir the sesame seeds occasionally so that they turn an even golden brown.

2. Place the sesame seeds, chickpeas, garlic, olive oil, and lemon juice in a blender or food processor and process for a few seconds until combined, but not too smooth. Transfer the hummus to a bowl and season to taste with freshly ground black pepper. Cover and chill.

3. Spoon the hummus into a serving dish and garnish with a sprig of parsley. Serve with strips of warm pita bread and bell peppers, celery, and cucumber.

Red Lentil Dal

MAKES ABOUT 1¾ CUPS

This mildly spiced dal makes an ideal dip for a packed lunch or a first course before a curry main meal.

1 Tbsp sunflower oil
1 medium onion, chopped fine
2 garlic cloves, crushed
1 inch piece fresh root ginger, peeled and chopped fine
1 tsp ground coriander
1 tsp ground cumin
1 tsp ground turmeric
6 oz dried red lentils
Chile powder
Strips of warm pita bread, crusty bread and strips of celery and cucumber

1. Heat the oil in a saucepan and sauté the onion, garlic, ginger, and spices over a moderate heat for three minutes, stirring occasionally and taking care not to burn the spices.

2. Add the red lentils and two cups of cold water. Bring to a boil and cook rapidly for ten minutes. Cover and simmer for another fifteen to twenty minutes, or until the lentils are tender. Drain well and leave to cool completely.

3. Place three-quarters of the lentil mixture into a blender or food processor and process for a few seconds, until smooth. Turn into a bowl and stir in the remaining lentils to give the dip some texture. Cover and chill.

4. Transfer the dal to a serving dish and sprinkle with a pinch of chile powder to garnish. Serve with strips of warm pita bread, crusty bread, and strips of celery and cucumber.

Hot Tex Mex Dip

MAKES ABOUT 1¼ CUPS

This hearty, colorful Mexican dip is a real feast. If you prefer your chili flavor really hot, then there is no need to deseed the chiles before chopping.

8 oz canned kidney beans, drained and rinsed
8 oz canned tomatoes, drained and chopped
2 green chiles, deseeded and chopped
3 Tbsp onion, chopped fine
½ small yellow bell pepper, deseeded and diced fine
½ small green bell pepper, deseeded and diced fine
Chunky strips of bell pepper, tortilla chips, and taco shells

1. Combine the kidney beans, tomatoes, chiles, onion, and yellow and green bell pepper. Cover and chill.

2. Transfer the dip into a serving bowl. Serve with strips of yellow, green, and red bell pepper cut wide enough to scoop up the chunky dip. Tortilla chips and taco shells are also suitable accompaniments.

Green Lentil and Spinach Dip

MAKES ABOUT 1½ CUPS

4 oz dried green lentils, rinsed and drained
4 oz fresh young spinach, washed and drained
⅔ cup plain yogurt
2 tsp hot curry powder
Chunky strips of pita bread and bell peppers

1. Place the lentils in a saucepan with two cups of cold water. Bring to a boil and cook rapidly for ten minutes. Cover and simmer for another fifteen to twenty minutes, or until tender. Drain and allow to cool completely.

2. Meanwhile, place the spinach in a large heatproof colander over a sink and pour over four cups of boiling water – this is all the cooking the spinach will require. Drain well and allow to cool completely. When the spinach is cool, squeeze out any excess water and cut it into fine shreds.

3. Blend the yogurt and curry powder together in a bowl. Stir in the cold lentils and spinach. Cover and chill.

4. Transfer the lentil dip into a serving bowl and serve with chunky pieces of pita bread and bell peppers to scoop up this hearty dip.

Curried Bean Dip

MAKES ABOUT 1½ CUPS

15 oz canned mixed beans, e.g. chickpeas, pinto,
black-eyed, kidney, drained and rinsed
½ cup plain yogurt
1 tsp hot curry powder
1 tsp lemon juice
Slices of lemon and a pinch of curry powder
Strips of warm pita bread and crusty bread

1. Blend the yogurt, curry powder, and lemon juice together. Stir in the beans. Cover and chill.

2. Transfer the dip to a serving bowl. Garnish with slices of lemon and sprinkle with the pinch of curry powder. Serve with wide strips of warm pita bread and crusty bread to scoop up this chunky dip.

Butter Bean Dip

MAKES ABOUT 1¼ CUPS

Butter beans have a creamy flavor that go well with fish to make a filling meal. Or, serve with vegetables as a lighter alternative.

15 oz canned butter beans, drained and rinsed
⅓ cup plain yogurt
½ small lemon, juice and rind, grated fine
2 Tbsp fresh parsley, chopped
Freshly ground black pepper
Baked or fried batter-coated fish nuggets or scampi
AND/OR strips of carrot, broccoli florets, and blanched
fine green beans

1. Place the butter beans and yogurt in a blender or food processor and process for a few seconds until smooth. Transfer the bean purée to a bowl.

2. Stir in the lemon juice and rind and parsley. Season well with freshly ground black pepper. Cover and chill.

3. Spoon the dip into a serving bowl and serve with warm, cooked batter-coated fish sticks for a substantial dip, or alternatively serve a selection of vegetables such as strips of carrot, broccoli florets, and blanched green beans.

Pesto Bean Dip

MAKES ABOUT 1¼ CUPS

Pesto sauce can be bought ready-made and has a distinctive basil flavor.

2 Tbsp pesto
15 oz canned Soya beans, drained and rinsed
⅓ cup plain yogurt
Tomato wedges, breadsticks, crusty bread, and olive bread, cubed

1. Place the pesto, beans, and yogurt in a blender or food processor and process for a few seconds until smooth. Transfer to a bowl, cover, and chill.
2. Spoon the dip into a serving bowl and serve with wedges of tomato, breadsticks, and cubes of crusty and olive bread.

Mexican Bean Dip

MAKES ABOUT 1¼ CUPS

15 oz canned red pinto beans, drained and rinsed
2 garlic cloves, crushed
3 Tbsp chopped onion
¼ tsp ground cumin
2 Tbsp olive oil
2 green chiles, deseeded and chopped fine
Strips of red, yellow, and green bell peppers, and tortilla chips

1. Place the beans, garlic, onion, cumin, and olive oil in a blender or food processor and process for a few seconds until smooth. Transfer to a bowl and stir in the chopped chiles. Cover and chill.
2. Spoon the dip into a serving bowl and serve with strips of red, yellow, and green bell peppers and tortilla chips.

Creamed Chickpea and Hazelnut Dip

MAKES ABOUT 1½ CUPS

Crunchy toasted hazelnut in creamy chickpeas makes an unusual and appetizing dip that is popular with vegetarians as a packed lunch or when served at a dinner party.

2 oz hazelnuts, chopped
15 oz canned chickpeas, drained and rinsed
⅔ cup heavy cream
2 Tbsp milk
Freshly ground black pepper
Cored apple wedges, strips of celery and cucumber and potato chips

1. Place the chopped hazelnuts in a single layer on a sheet of aluminum foil on a baking tray. Toast under a moderate, preheated broiler for about two to three minutes, turning occasionally, until they turn a golden brown. Take care that they don't brown too suddenly. Remove from the heat and leave to cool completely.
2. Place the chickpeas, cream, and milk in a blender or food processor and process for a few seconds until smooth.
3. Turn the chickpea mixture into a bowl. Reserve one tablespoon of the toasted hazelnuts and stir the remaining nuts into the chickpea mixture. Season well with freshly ground black pepper. Cover and chill.
4. Spoon the dip into a serving bowl and sprinkle with the reserved hazelnuts. Serve with cored apple wedges (dipped in lemon juice to prevent discoloring), strips of celery and cucumber, and potato chips.

FRUIT DIPS –
SAVORY AND SWEET

6

Cranberry and Orange Dip with Herbed Crumb-coated Turkey Sticks

MAKES ABOUT 1¼ CUPS

Thanksgiving and Christmas are ideal occasions for serving this festive dip with strips of turkey coated in parsley- and thyme-flavored bread crumbs for added crunch and flavor.

FOR THE DIP
14 oz cranberries
2 large oranges, juice and rind, grated fine
3 oz fine granulated sugar
Salt and freshly ground black pepper

FOR THE TURKEY STICKS
1 lb skinless and boneless turkey breast meat
2 eggs, beaten
¾ cup dried bread crumb stuffing mix, e.g. parsley and thyme
Vegetable oil for deep frying

1. Place the cranberries, orange juice, and one-quarter cup cold water in a large saucepan. Reserve one teaspoon of the orange rind for a garnish and add the remaining rind to the cranberries. *Slowly* bring to a boil, cover, and simmer for about fifteen to twenty minutes, until the cranberries are tender. As the cranberries come to a boil, take care not to get burned by hot cranberry juice. This can be reduced by heating slowly.

2. Remove the cooked cranberries from the heat. Stir in the sugar until it has dissolved completely. Allow the dip to cool.

3. Pour the cranberry mixture into a blender or food processor and process for a few seconds until smooth. Spoon the purée into a fine nylon sieve over a bowl and press through the purée to remove the cranberry skins. Season to taste, and cover the sieved cranberry dip and chill.

4. To make the Turkey Sticks: Cut the turkey breast meat into one-half inch by two inch strips. Dip the turkey strips, a few at a time, into the beaten eggs and then into the herbed bread crumb mixture. Deep fry, in batches, in oil preheated to 355°F for about five minutes or until the crumbs are golden and crisp and the turkey is thoroughly cooked. Drain on paper towels and keep warm while cooking the remaining batches.

5. Transfer the dip to a serving dish and sprinkle with the reserved orange rind. Serve with the warm turkey sticks.

Apricot and Mango Chutney Dip

MAKES ABOUT 1½ CUPS

Serve this dip with warm samosas and onion rings for a real feast.

7 oz dried apricots
5 whole green cardamoms
3 Tbsp mango chutney
Samosas and onion rings

1. Place the dried apricots in a large bowl and cover with two cups of cold water. Leave to soak overnight.

2. Place the soaked apricots in a saucepan with the soaking water and green cardamoms. Bring to a boil, cover, and simmer for forty minutes. Allow

the cooked apricots to cool completely in the liquid.

3. Drain the apricots. Remove the cardamoms. Place the apricots in a blender or food processor and process for a few seconds until smooth.

4. Transfer the apricot purée to a bowl and stir in the mango chutney. Cover and chill.

5. Transfer the dip to a serving bowl and serve with samosas and onion rings.

Pineapple, Avocado, and Red Onion Salsa

MAKES ABOUT 1¼ CUPS

8 oz canned pineapple in natural juice
1 red onion, chopped fine
1 green chile, deseeded and chopped
1 medium avocado
2 Tbsp fresh coriander, chopped
Freshly ground black pepper
Tortilla chips, nachos, and pita bread cut into wide strips

1. Drain the pineapple, reserving the juice. Chop the pineapple into small pieces.

2. Cut the avocado in half lengthwise and twist the halves in opposite directions to pull the two halves apart. Remove the pit and skin. Finely dice the avocado flesh and toss in the reserved pineapple juice to prevent discoloration.

3. Combine all of the ingredients in a bowl and season well with freshly ground black pepper. Cover and chill.

4. Transfer the salsa to a serving dish and serve with tortilla chips, nachos, and pita bread cut in strips wide enough so that the chunky salsa can be scooped up.

Pineapple and Chive Cheese Dip

MAKES ABOUT 1¼ CUPS

The hollowed-out pineapple shells make ideal containers in which to serve this dip. It's best to serve it fairly soon after making; on standing the fresh pineapple exudes juice that can make the dip too moist.

1 small, ripe pineapple
½ cup cottage cheese
2 Tbsp plain yogurt
2 Tbsp fresh chives, chopped
Pinch of paprika
Freshly ground black pepper
Fresh chives, chopped
A selection of crackers, strips of celery, cucumber, and carrot

1. Cut the pineapple in half lengthwise. With a sharp knife carefully cut around the inner edge of the pineapple halves and scoop out the flesh with a spoon.

2. Place the empty pineapple halves upside down on a deep plate to allow excess juice to run out. Cover and chill.

3. Cut the pineapple flesh into small chunks. Place the pieces in a sieve over a bowl and allow any excess juice to drain away.

4. Combine the cottage cheese with the yogurt in a bowl. Stir in the pineapple chunks, chives, and paprika. Season to taste with freshly ground black pepper. Cover and chill.

5. Just before serving, spoon the dip into the pineapple halves and garnish with chopped chives. Serve with a selection of crackers and strips of celery, cucumber, and carrot.

Curried Mango Dip

Mango and Indian spices make an unusual and tasty dip, which never fails to impress.

1 medium, ripe mango (you require about 7 oz flesh)
2 Tbsp mango chutney
1 tsp medium hot curry paste OR ½ tsp medium hot curry powder
½ cup whole plain yogurt
Fresh sprigs of coriander
Crusty bread, pita bread cut into strips; cucumber and red bell pepper strips

1. Cut down either side of the large, flat mango pit with a sharp knife to remove the flesh. Using a vegetable peeler or sharp knife, remove the mango skin. Roughly chop the mango and place in a blender or food processor and process for a few seconds until smooth.

2. Turn the mango purée into a mixing bowl and stir in the mango chutney, curry paste or powder, and yogurt. Cover and chill.

3. Transfer the dip to a serving dish and garnish with fresh coriander leaves. Serve with a selection of crusty breads, strips of pita bread, cucumber, and red bell pepper.

Papaya, Mango, and Pomegranate Salsa

MAKES ABOUT 1¼ CUPS

This chunky, colorful salsa wakes up tired taste buds with its fruity and fiery flavors.

1 small, ripe mango
1 medium, ripe papaya
1 pomegranate
1 small onion, chopped fine
2 green chiles, deseeded and chopped fine
1 Tbsp fresh coriander, chopped
Freshly ground black pepper
Tortilla chips and wide strips of red, yellow, and green bell peppers

1. Cut down each side of the large, central pit in the mango with a sharp knife to remove the flesh. With a vegetable peeler or sharp knife, remove the mango skin. Finely dice the mango and place in a bowl.

2. Prepare the papaya by cutting in half lengthwise and scooping out the black seeds with a spoon. Remove the skin with a vegetable peeler or sharp knife. Cut the papaya flesh into finely diced pieces and add to the mango.

3. Lightly roll the pomegranate with your hand on a kitchen surface to loosen the fruit inside. Cut the pomegranate in half and carefully pick out the pieces of pomegranate from the husk and add to the mango and papaya.

4. Add the prepared onion, chiles, and coriander to the fruit and mix thoroughly. Season well with freshly ground black pepper. Cover and chill.

5. Transfer the salsa to a serving dish. Serve with foods suitable for scooping up the chunky texture of the salsa, such as tortilla chips and wide strips of red, yellow, and green bell peppers.

Kiwi Cream Dip

MAKES ABOUT 1½ CUPS

3 ripe kiwis
1 Tbsp apricot brandy
⅔ cup plain yogurt
Small wedges of peeled mango, papaya, and banana

1. Trim off the ends of the kiwis and remove the skin with a sharp knife or vegetable peeler. Reserve a few slices for decoration and roughly chop the remaining fruit. Place in a blender or food processor and process until smooth.
2. Pour the purée into a bowl and stir in the apricot brandy. Lightly swirl in the yogurt. Cover and chill.
3. To serve, decorate with the reserved kiwi slices. Serve with small wedges of peeled mango, papaya, and banana (dipped in lime juice to prevent discoloring).

Strawberry Dream Dip

MAKES ABOUT 1¼ CUPS

5 oz strawberries, hulled
2 Tbsp powdered sugar
1 cup plain yogurt
Wedges of pear, peach, and banana OR marshmallows, mini doughnuts, and mini sweet muffins

1. Place the strawberries in a small processor or blender and process for a few seconds until smooth. Transfer the purée to a fine nylon sieve set over a small bowl and with a spoon or press the purée through the sieve to remove the seeds.
2. Stir the powdered sugar into the strawberry purée and then blend in the yogurt until smooth. Cover and chill.

3. Turn the dip into a serving dish. For health-conscious diners, serve with wedges of cored pear, peach, and banana (coated in lime or lemon juice to prevent discoloring), or, for a more wicked feast, try dipping marshmallows, mini doughnuts, and mini sweet muffins. Delicious!

Blueberry Swirl Dip

MAKES ABOUT 1¼ CUPS

Serve this dip soon after lightly swirling the blueberries and yogurt together or else the blueberry color "bleeds" into the white and the dip's stunning appearance is lost (although it still tastes as good!)

9 oz blueberries, fresh or frozen
2 tsp arrowroot
⅓ cup plain yogurt
Peeled and cored pear wedges, and chocolate and vanilla sponge cake

1. Place the blueberries in a saucepan with one-quarter cup cold water. Bring to a boil and simmer for five minutes, until tender.
2. Blend the arrowroot in a small cup with two tablespoons cold water. Stir one tablespoon of the hot blueberry liquid into the arrowroot, then pour the blended mixture into the blueberries and stir well. Return to a boil, stirring continuously, until thickened (this should only take seconds). Remove the pan from the heat and allow to cool completely. Chill in the refrigerator until just about to serve.
3. Pour the blueberry mixture into a serving bowl and lightly swirl in the yogurt. Serve with peeled and cored wedges of pear (which have been dipped in lemon juice to prevent discoloring) and chocolate and vanilla sponge cake cut into cubes.

Cinnamon and Raisin Yogurt Dip with Apple Fritters

MAKES ABOUT 1¼ CUPS

Serve this dip with warm apple fritters for best effect, but if you don't have time to make them then wedges of cored apple can be served instead. Calvados is a brandy made from apples – if you don't have any, use cider or apple juice to plump up the raisins.

FOR THE DIP
3 oz raisins
3 Tbsp Calvados
1 cup plain yogurt
½ tsp ground cinnamon

FOR THE APPLE FRITTERS
1 quantity of batter (see Quick Tomato Dip with Turkey Sticks, page 28 for batter recipe)
5 large eating apples
Vegetable oil, for deep frying
Dusting of powdered sugar, for dredging over cooked apple fritters

1. To make the Dip: In a small bowl, soak the raisins in the Calvados for at least two hours or preferably overnight. Then combine all of the dip ingredients, cover, and chill.

2. To make the Apple Fritters: Heat the oil for frying to 375°F. Peel and core the apples. Cut the apples into rings about one-quarter inch thick. When the oil is up to temperature, dip the apple rings into the batter, shake off the excess, and carefully place them in the hot oil. Cook a few at a time, turning them over when one side is golden brown. When completely golden, remove with a slotted spoon and drain on paper towels. Keep warm while cooking the remaining apple rings.

3. Dredge the warm apple fritters with powdered sugar and serve immediately with the dip.

Autumnal Fruits with Port Dip

MAKES ABOUT 1¼ CUPS

There is something warming and comforting about this dip – its rich, luscious colors and indescribable flavor make you go back for more and more. While it can be served warm or chilled, I like to serve it warm at bonfire night parties. Make sure you have plenty of dipping accompaniments to serve with it.

11 oz mixed berries, e.g. red currants, black currants,
raspberries, blackberries (fresh or frozen)
⅔ cup port
3 Tbsp superfine sugar
4 tsp arrowroot
Cored apple wedges, mini sweet muffins, lady fingers,
and marshmallows

1. Place the berries in a saucepan with one-quarter cup of the port and the sugar. Bring to a boil and simmer uncovered for ten minutes.
2. Blend the arrowroot with the remaining port. Add two tablespoons of the hot berry mixture to the blended arrowroot, then pour the mixture back into the saucepan. Return to a boil, stirring continuously, until thickened.
3. If serving hot, pour into a heatproof serving dish immediately, or allow to cool completely, then cover and chill in the refrigerator until required. Serve the dip with apples cored and cut into wedges (dipped in lemon juice to prevent discoloring), mini sweet muffins, lady fingers, and marshmallows.

Butterscotch Dip with Broiled Bananas

MAKES ABOUT 1 CUP
SERVES 4 PEOPLE AS A DESSERT

This dip is extremely sweet but delicious. It's a dip that has to be served warm and I particularly like to serve it with banana slices that have been warmed under the broiler.

⅔ cup pourable honey
6 Tbsp butter
¼ cup dark brown sugar
4 large bananas, ripe but firm
Juice of 1 lemon

1. Place the honey, butter, and brown sugar in a small saucepan and heat very gently, stirring occasionally, until the butter and sugar have completely dissolved in the honey. Take care not to boil the mixture. Keep it on a low heat to stay warm while the bananas are prepared.
2. Peel the bananas and cut in half lengthwise. Cut each half of the banana into thirds and dip in the lemon juice. Place the banana pieces under a hot preheated broiler for just long enough to warm them through – only a couple of minutes. Take care not to cook them too long or they suddenly go soft and then can't be dipped into the Butterscotch Dip. (If this does happen then never fear, the dip can be served poured over the bananas – as I have done a few times when I've been too busy chatting with my guests!)
3. Serve the butterscotch dip in individual ramekins placed on a plate with the broiled bananas arranged around the side.

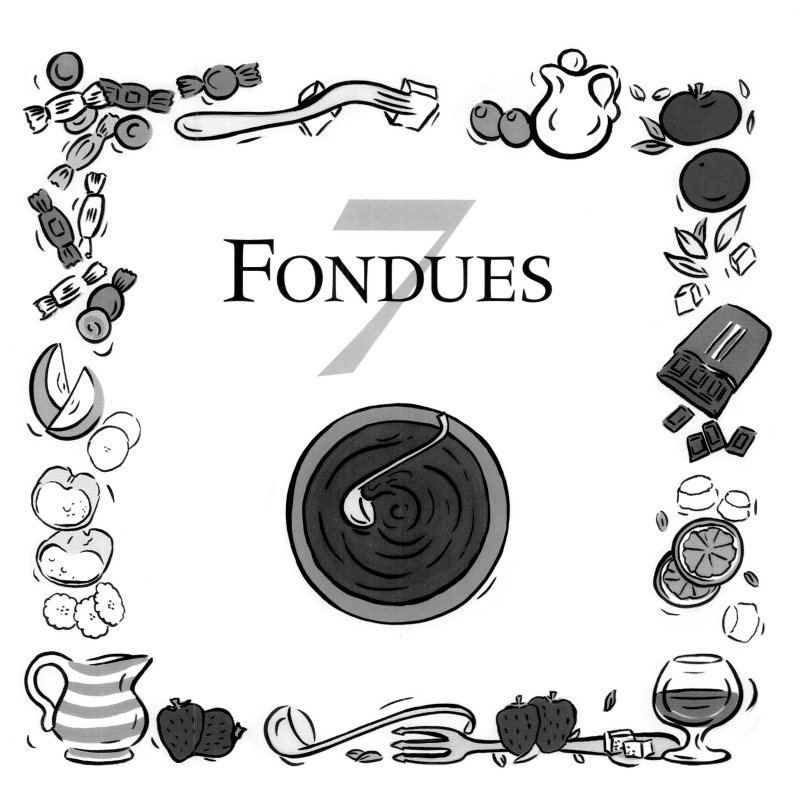

FONDUES

7

Fondues are often considered the ultimate dips – they are always served warm and often contain alcohol.

They are great dips for an informal meal or supper with friends when you can sit and chat, relaxing and idly dipping into the fondue. It has been said that fondues make ideal party food, since if a person drops a piece of food from their fork into the fondue, they then have to carry out a forfeit – I'll leave those forfeit suggestions to your imagination. Whenever you have your fondue, simply have fun and enjoy.

Don't worry if you haven't got a fondue set, you can still keep your fondue warm by pouring it into a warmed heatproof dish over a tabletop warmer with nightlights. Long-handled fondue forks do help with the dipping, but ordinary forks or skewers can be used as an alternative.

The savory fondues in this chapter make about two and one-half cups, which will serve six to eight people for a first course or four people as a main course when accompanied with plenty of dipping foods.

The sweet fondues make about one and one-quarter cups, which should serve four to six people as a dessert, since they are very rich. However, if you fancy a sweet dip with no other courses, then double up the ingredients.

The secret to successful fondues is the very slow melting of the ingredients over a very low heat, so that they combine thoroughly without separating or burning on the base of the pan. Be patient – don't rush this stage and you will be rewarded with a beautifully smooth fondue dip. Also warm the serving dish in which you will serve the fondue, especially for the cheese fondues: If they cool the cheese starts to reset and becomes too thick and stringy for dipping. However, if this does occur, do not fear; just gently reheat the fondue mixture.

Cider and Cheese Fondue

MAKES ABOUT 2½ CUPS

12 oz Gruyère cheese, grated fine
1 garlic clove, crushed fine
1 cup plus 1 Tbsp medium dry cider
1 Tbsp cornstarch
Freshly ground black pepper
Cored wedges of apple, cubes of crusty bread,
strips of cooked ham, chunks of cucumber and celery,
and tomato wedges

1. Place the cheese, garlic, and one cup of the cider in a heavy-bottom saucepan and heat very gently, until the cheese has completely melted into the cider – this will take about twenty minutes. Stir the mixture occasionally.

2. When the cheese has melted, in a bowl blend the cornstarch with the remaining cider and add two tablespoons of the hot fondue mixture. Immediately return the mixture to the pan and stir well. Season well with freshly ground black pepper.

3. Pour the fondue into a warmed, heatproof serving dish. Keep the fondue warm over a fondue holder or tabletop warmer with nightlights. Serve with plenty of dipping accompaniments such as cored apple wedges (dipped in lemon juice to prevent discoloring), cubes of crusty bread, strips of cooked ham, chunks of celery and cucumber, and tomato wedges.

Double Cheese Fondue

MAKES ABOUT 2½ CUPS

6 oz Gruyère cheese, grated fine
6 oz Emmanthal cheese, grated fine
1 cup plus 1 Tbsp dry white wine
1 Tbsp cornstarch
Freshly ground black pepper
Cubes of crusty bread, small breadsticks, cheese straws,
diced bell peppers, tomato wedges, and sliced raw zucchini

1. Place the cheeses and one cup of the wine into a heavy-bottom saucepan and heat very gently, until the cheese has completely melted into the wine – this will take about twenty minutes. Stir the mixture occasionally.

2. When the cheese has melted, in a bowl blend the cornstarch with the remaining wine, add two tablespoons of the hot fondue, and immediately return the mixture to the pan, stirring thoroughly. Season well with freshly ground black pepper.

3. Pour the fondue into a warmed, heatproof serving dish and place over a fondue holder or tabletop warmer with nightlights. Serve with plenty of dipping accompaniments such as cubed crusty bread, breadsticks, cheese straws, diced peppers, tomato wedges, and slices of raw zucchini.

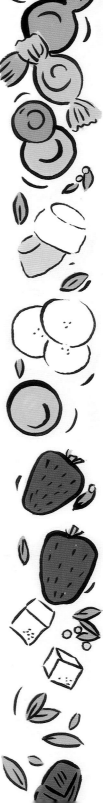

Devil's Chocolate Fondue

MAKES ABOUT 1¼ CUPS

7 oz milk chocolate, broken into small cubes
4 Tbsp butter
¼ cup milk
3 Tbsp brandy
Cubes of sponge cake, mini sweet muffins,
mini doughnuts, and cookies

1. Place the chocolate, butter, and milk in a small, heavy-bottom saucepan and heat very gently, until the ingredients have completely melted and combined thoroughly – this will take about fifteen minutes. Stir occasionally.
2. Stir in the brandy. Pour into a warmed, heatproof serving dish and keep warm over a fondue holder or a tabletop warmer with nightlights. Serve with cubed pieces of sponge cake, mini sweet muffins, mini doughnuts and cookies for dipping.

Marshmallow Delight Fondue

MAKES ABOUT 1¼ CUPS

7 oz mini white marshmallows
⅓ cup condensed milk
2 Tbsp milk
Seedless grapes, sliced bananas and peaches,
and strawberries

1. Place the marshmallows, condensed milk, and milk into a small, heavy-bottom saucepan and heat very slowly, until the marshmallows have completely melted and combined with the other ingredients. This will take about fifteen to twenty minutes – a very low heat is required to prevent the marshmallow from burning on the base of the pan. Stir the mixture occasionally.
2. Pour the marshmallow fondue into a warmed, heatproof serving dish and keep warm over a fondue holder or a tabletop warmer with nightlights. Serve with seedless grapes, sliced bananas and peaches (both dipped in lemon juice to prevent discoloring), and strawberries for dipping.

Fresh Tomato and Basil Fondue

MAKES ABOUT 2½ CUPS

2 lb large, ripe tomatoes
1 Tbsp olive oil
1 small onion, chopped fine
1 garlic clove, crushed
⅓ cup dry white wine
1 tsp fine granulated sugar
Freshly ground black pepper
2 Tbsp fresh basil, chopped
Cubed crusty garlic bread, shelled, cooked jumbo shrimp, diced bell peppers, and chunks of celery

1. Skin the tomatoes by cutting a small cross in the base of each tomato with a sharp knife then place them in a heatproof bowl and pour over boiling water. Leave for a few seconds and you should see the skins loosen and start to peel away. Drain in a colander and cool under cold running water. Remove the skins, then chop the tomatoes into wedges and discard the seeds. Finely chop the remaining tomato flesh.
2. Heat the oil in a saucepan and gently sauté the onion and garlic for five minutes, until softened but not browned.
3. Add the chopped tomato and slowly bring to a boil. Simmer, uncovered, for about twenty to thirty minutes so that the tomato mixture can reduce and thicken.
4. Remove from the heat, stir in the wine and sugar. Season to taste with freshly ground black pepper. Pour the tomato fondue into a warmed heatproof serving dish and keep warm over a fondue holder or on a tabletop warmer with nightlights. Sprinkle with the chopped basil. Serve with plenty of dipping accompaniments such as cubed crusty garlic bread, shelled, cooked jumbo shrimp, diced bell peppers, and chunks of celery.

Creamy Toffee Fondue with Popcorn

MAKES ABOUT 1¼ CUPS

Use creamy toffee rather than a brittle toffee when making this fondue.

7 oz creamy toffee candy
4 Tbsp butter
¼ cup milk
Plain unsalted or unsweetened popcorn

1. Place the toffees, butter, and milk in a small, heavy-bottom saucepan and heat very gently, until the ingredients have completely melted and combined thoroughly – this will take about fifteen minutes. Stir the mixture occasionally.
2. Carefully pour the very hot toffee fondue into a warmed, heatproof serving dish and keep warm over a fondue holder or tabletop warmer with nightlights. Serve with freshly made, warm, unsalted, and unsweetened popcorn, using cocktail sticks to dip the popcorn into the toffee fondue.

MORE & FAVORITES

Peppery Mayonnaise Dip

MAKES ABOUT 1¼ CUPS

1 cup mayonnaise
4 shallots, chopped fine
2 Tbsp fresh chives, chopped fine
2 Tbsp white whole peppercorns
Hot sauce
Strips of celery, carrot, cucumber, zucchini, and blanched
baby sweetcorn

1. Mix together the mayonnaise, shallots, and chives in a bowl.
2. Lightly crush the peppercorns in a pestle and mortar, or place in a small plastic bag and crush lightly with a rolling pin. Stir the peppercorns into the dip mixture.
3. Add as many drops of hot sauce as your taste prefers. Five to six drops are recommended, since the flavor matures and seems to strengthen upon chilling the dip. Cover and chill.
4. Spoon the dip into a serving bowl. Serve with strips of raw celery, carrot, cucumber, zucchini, and blanched and cooled baby sweetcorn.

Caper and Gherkin Dip

MAKES ABOUT 1½ CUPS

1 cup lowfat plain yogurt
2 Tbsp capers, chopped fine
3 oz pickled gherkins, chopped fine
2 Tbsp fresh tarragon, chopped fine
Freshly ground black pepper
Fresh tarragon sprigs
Strips of red, yellow, and green bell peppers, zucchini,
and celery

1. Combine the yogurt, capers, gherkins, and tarragon. Season well with freshly ground black pepper. Cover and chill.
2. Transfer the dip to a serving dish and garnish with sprigs of tarragon. Serve with strips of red, yellow, and green bell peppers, zucchini, and celery.

Whole-grain Mustard Dip

MAKES ABOUT 1¼ CUPS

1 cup mayonnaise
⅓ cup plain yogurt
3 Tbsp whole-grain OR coarse-grain mustard
1 tsp English mustard
Freshly ground black pepper
Deep-fried or baked batter-coated vegetables, e.g. onion
rings, and strips of eggplant and zucchini

1. Place the mayonnaise, yogurt, and mustards in a bowl and mix thoroughly. Season to taste with freshly ground black pepper. Cover and chill.
2. Spoon the dip into a serving dish and serve with warm deep-fried or baked chunks of batter-coated mixed vegetables, such as onion rings, and strips of eggplant and zucchini.

Egg and Parsley Dip

MAKES ABOUT 1½ CUPS

3 hard-boiled eggs, chilled and shelled
⅔ cup mayonnaise
1 Tbsp milk
5 Tbsp fresh parsley, chopped fine
Freshly ground black pepper
Sprig of fresh parsley
Strips of white and brown bread, toasted

1. Place the hard-boiled eggs in a bowl and with the back of a fork mash them into fine pieces.
2. Stir thoroughly the mayonnaise and milk into the eggs. Add the fresh parsley and season well with freshly ground black pepper. Cover and chill.
3. Spoon the dip into a serving bowl and garnish with a sprig of fresh parsley. Serve with toasted strips of white and brown bread.

Fresh Herbed Yogurt Dip

MAKES ABOUT 1¼ CUPS

1 cup whole plain yogurt
2 oz mixed fresh herbs, e.g. chives, parsley, oregano, thyme,
and marjoram
Freshly ground black pepper
Fish, meat, and vegetable kabobs, barbecued or broiled,
and a selection of vegetable crudités

1. Place the yogurt in a bowl.
2. Remove any large or woody stalks from the herbs and chop the leaves fine. Add to the yogurt and mix thoroughly. Season well with freshly ground black pepper. Cover and chill.
3. Transfer the dip to a serving bowl. Serve with kabobs, fish, meat, and vegetables (barbecued or broiled), and a selection of vegetable crudités.

Tofu and Peanut Butter Dip

MAKES ABOUT 1½ CUPS

½ cup smooth peanut butter
⅓ cup milk
7 oz firm tofu, drained
1 tsp tomato paste
Cayenne pepper
2 Tbsp roasted peanuts, chopped
Toasted strips of bread, and bell peppers

1. Place the peanut butter in a bowl. In a small saucepan, gently heat the milk until warm but not boiling. Gradually blend the milk into the peanut butter to make a smooth soft paste – I find this is best done with a fork. Allow to cool.
2. Place the tofu in a separate bowl with the tomato paste and with a fork blend together. The tofu will readily break up into a smooth mash.
3. Combine the peanut butter and tofu mixtures and season to taste with cayenne pepper. Remember cayenne is very hot, so add sparingly. Cover and chill.
4. Spoon the dip into a serving bowl and sprinkle with the chopped peanuts. Serve with strips of toasted bread and bell peppers.

Tofu and Sesame Dip

MAKES ABOUT 1¼ CUPS

Tofu or solid bean curd can be found in health food stores and most supermarkets. Before using tofu, drain away the excess liquid it is packed in. Tahini, also found in health food stores, has a strong sesame flavor.

1 Tbsp sesame seeds
11 oz firm tofu, drained
1 Tbsp lemon juice
1 Tbsp light tahini
1 tsp sesame oil
1 garlic clove, crushed
1 tsp cider vinegar
2 scallions, chopped fine
Strips of celery, cucumber, bell peppers, and carrot; small florets of broccoli and cauliflower

1. Place the sesame seeds in a single layer on a piece of aluminum foil on a baking tray. Toast under a moderate preheated broiler for about two to three minutes, turning occasionally, until they turn a pale golden brown. Take care that the seeds don't brown too suddenly. Remove from the heat and allow to cool completely.
2. Place the tofu, lemon juice, tahini, sesame oil, garlic, and vinegar in a blender or food processor and process for a few seconds, until smooth. Transfer to a bowl and stir in three-quarters of the chopped scallions. Reserve the remaining scallion as a garnish. Cover and chill.
3. Transfer the dip to a serving bowl and sprinkle with the sesame seeds and reserved chopped scallion. Serve with strips of celery, cucumber, bell peppers, and carrot and small florets of broccoli and cauliflower.

Creamy Egg Brunch Dip

MAKES ABOUT 1¼ CUPS

This delicious dip makes an ideal brunch on weekends when you have visiting guests and could also be served at a "working breakfast," where it's bound to impress! Serves four to six when accompanied with plenty of cooked cocktail sausages, bacon strips, smoked salmon rolled up into bite sized pieces, and tomato wedges. Serve also with toast, warm crusty bread, and plenty of coffee or tea.

6 eggs
⅔ cup heavy cream
Salt and freshly ground black pepper
2 Tbsp butter
2 Tbsp fresh chives, chopped
Cooked cocktail sausages, fried bacon strips, thinly sliced smoked salmon (cut and rolled up), tomato wedges, toast, and crusty bread

1. Beat the eggs with the cream in a bowl. Season with salt and pepper.
2. Melt the butter in a large (if possible, nonstick) frying pan until it gently sizzles. Pour in the egg mixture and cook over a moderately low heat, stirring continuously, until cooked, about six to seven minutes. The eggs should have a creamy, smooth, scrambled-egg appearance.
3. Transfer the egg dip to a serving bowl and sprinkle with the chopped chives. Serve with the cooked cocktail sausages, bacon strips, small rolled-up slices of smoked salmon, tomato wedges, toast, and crusty bread. Enjoy while warm.

Garlic Dip

MAKES ABOUT 1¼ CUPS

The base for this dip is homemade mayonnaise, which can be used in any of the other recipes requiring mayonnaise. However, if you are concerned about eating raw eggs, then use ready-made mayonnaise, made from pasteurized eggs. As ever, the secret to making a successful mayonnaise is patience – add the oil very gradually and beat each addition in well before adding any more. If the oil is added too quickly, it will fail to emulsify and the mixture will separate. Using a blender or food processor has taken all the hard work out of beating the oil in by hand.

2 egg yolks
½ tsp salt
¼ tsp mustard powder
¼ tsp ground white pepper
¼ tsp fine granulated sugar
½ cup olive oil
½ cup sunflower oil
1 Tbsp lemon juice
4 garlic cloves, crushed
Strips of carrot, celery, cucumber, and bell peppers;
small broccoli and cauliflower florets

1. Place the egg yolks, salt, mustard, pepper, and sugar in a blender or food processor and blend on high speed for about fifteen seconds.
2. Reduce the speed to medium and initially add the oil, drop by drop, through the hole in the lid. As the oil is blended into the egg yolks, very slowly drizzle the oil into the mixture, blending until a smooth mayonnaise has been made. Add the lemon juice and garlic then transfer to a bowl, cover, and chill.

3. Spoon the dip into a serving bowl and surround with strips of carrot, celery, cucumber, and bell peppers, and small florets of broccoli and cauliflower.

Tahini Dip

MAKES ABOUT 1¼ CUPS

Tahini is made from sesame seeds and has a very distinctive flavor. Although this dip looks very thin when first made, once chilled it thickens to a good dipping consistency.

¼ cup light tahini
⅔ cup plain yogurt
¼ cup unsweetened apple juice
1 tsp cider vinegar
1 garlic clove, crushed (optional)
Freshly ground black pepper
Cored apple wedges, strips of celery, and chips

1. Soften the tahini in a bowl with a spoon so that the yogurt will blend in more readily. Add the yogurt and mix well.
2. Stir in the apple juice, cider vinegar, and garlic, if using. Season well with freshly ground black pepper to taste. Cover and chill.
3. Spoon the dip into a serving dish and serve with cored apple wedges (dipped in lemon juice to prevent discoloring), strips of celery, and potato chips.

WHAT GOES WITH WHAT

WHAT GOES WITH WHAT

The charts here and on the following pages show at a glance the variety of dips and the accompaniments well suited to them as dipping foods. Feel free to experiment. The chart can be used as inspiration for other serving ideas.

CHEESE DIPS	ACCOMPANIMENTS				
	VEGETABLE	FRUIT	SEAFOOD	BREADS	SNACKS
Beer and Cheddar Dip	trimmed scallions			breadsticks	potato chips
Blue Cheese Dip	celery strips, florets of cauliflower and broccoli				
Brie and Pear Dip		small wedges of cantaloupe and watermelon			
Cheese and Pimento Dip				breadsticks	tortilla and potato chips
Cottage Cheese and Caper Dip	strips of red, green, yellow bell peppers, raddichio leaves		fish sticks		
Cream Cheese and Chive Dip	red onion wedges, celery, carrot and bell pepper strips				
Dill, Yogurt, and Cream Cheese Dip	fennel, endive, cucumber strips		fish sticks		
Edam Dip	quartered button mushrooms, tomato wedges, broccoli florets, carrot strips				
Green Olive and Cream Cheese Dip				breadsticks, warm pita bread strips	
Mountain High Dip	celery, cucumber, carrot strips			chunks of crusty bread	
Peppercorn Cheese Dip	cucumber and carrot strips			breadsticks	cheese straws
Pistachio and Blue Cheese Dip	celery strips	cored apple wedges		crusty bread	
Ricotta and Cream Walnut Dip	celery strips	cored apple wedges		cubed bagels	
Smoked Cheese Dip	tomato wedges, cucumber strips			toasted cubed bread	crackers

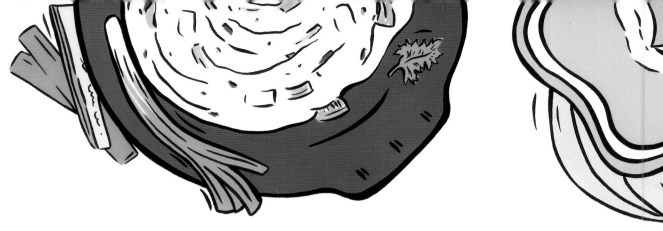

FISH DIPS	ACCOMPANIMENTS			
	VEGETABLE	SEAFOOD	BREAD	SNACKS
Avocado and Tuna Dip	zucchini and carrot strips, blanched fine			cheese straws
Bagna Cauda	green beans fennel, celery, carrot strips		cubed crusty bread	
Caper and Tartar Dip	strips of bell peppers, crisp lettuce leaves	fish sticks		
Chive and Smoked Oyster Dip			melba toast	
Crab Dip				potato chips, salty snacks
Creamy Caviar Dip			melba toast	
Creamy Tuna Dip	celery and cucumber strips, baby sweet corn, tomato wedges			
Deviled Egg and Tuna Dip	celery strips		toasted garlic bread	tortilla chips
Quick Anchovy Dip	green and black olives, quartered button mushrooms, bell pepper strips		chunks of Ciabatta or olive bread	
Shrimp Cocktail Dip	crisp lettuce leaves, celery and cucumber strips		melba toast	
Smoked Mackerel and Horseradish Dip			toasted triangles of white and brown bread	
Smoked Salmon and Lemon Dip	cucumber, celery, carrot strips		melba toast	
Taramasalata			warm pita bread strips	
Thai Coconut and Chile Crab Dip	trimmed scallions, strips of red bell pepper, cucumber, carrot			rice and shrimp crackers

MEAT DIPS	ACCOMPANIMENTS				
	VEGETABLE	**FRUIT**	**MEAT**	**BREAD**	**SNACKS**
Beef and Creamed Horseradish Dip	tomato wedges, crisp lettuce leaves, French fries				
Chicken and Almond Dip	cucumber, carrot, bell peppers, zucchini strips			cubed bagels or crusty bread	
Chicken Liver and Mushroom Dip				melba toast, rye bread	crackers
Chorizo Sausage and Tomato Dip				chunks of crusty bread or garlic bread	
Ham and Gruyère Dip	cucumber, celery, and carrot strips				
Peanut Satay Style Dip	cucumber and bell pepper strips, trimmed scallions		stir-fried pork strips – see recipe on page 27		
Quick Tangy Tomato Dip	French fries, celery, cucumber, zucchini strips		batter-coated turkey dipping sticks – see recipe on page 28		
Roasted Peanut and Ham Dip	celery, cucumber and carrot strips, tomato wedges			breadsticks	potato chips, crackers
Smoked Ham and Pineapple Dip		wedges of mango, papaya, melon			
Smoky Bacon and Cream Cheese Dip	celery strips			breadsticks	selection of crackers

VEGETABLE DIPS	ACCOMPANIMENTS				
	VEGETABLE	**SEAFOOD**	**MEAT**	**BREAD**	**SNACKS**
Black Olive Dip				wedges of olive bread or Ciabatta	
Butternut Squash Dip	fried or oven-roasted sweet potato wedges				
Cucumber and Lime Raita	cucumber and celery strips			warm pita bread strips, crusty bread	
Guacamole	bell pepper strips				tortilla chips
Mushroom and Pine Nut Dip				strips of crusty bread	selection of crackers
Puréed Vegetable and Pumpkin Seed Dip				wedges of breads, e.g. Ciabatta, tomato, olive, pumpernickel	
Radish Dip	crisp lettuce leaves, cucumber and celery strips	cooked, peeled jumbo shrimp			
Scallion Dip	crisp lettuce leaves, zucchini and bell pepper strips				potato chips
Scarlet Delight Dip	fennel, celery, zucchini, cucumber strips				
Smooth Chile Tomato Dip	deep-fried batter-coated vegetables (e.g. onion rings, cauliflower and broccoli florets), bell pepper strips	cooked, peeled jumbo shrimp		pita bread strips	
Sweet and Sour Dip	celery, cucumber, carrot, yellow and red bell pepper strips, canned water chestnuts, blanched and chilled baby sweet corn and snow peas				shrimp crackers
Tomato and Chile Salsa	wide strips of red, yellow, green, orange bell peppers				tortilla chips
Tzatziki	pan-fried strips of zucchini				

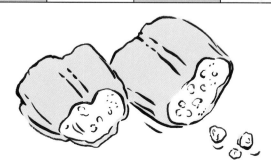

VEGETABLE DIPS	ACCOMPANIMENTS (CONTINUED)				
	VEGETABLE	SEAFOOD	MEAT	BREAD	SNACKS
Artichoke Heart Dip	broiled vegetables, e.g. red and yellow bell pepper, zucchini and eggplant strips				
Asparagus Cream Dip	chilled, cooked young asparagus tips and fine green beans; endive				
Celery and Spinach Dip					selection of small cheese crackers
Creamy Corn Dip	cucumber, carrot, celery strips			cubed bagels	cheese straws
Eggplant and Pepper Dip				warm slices of crusty garlic bread	
Quick and Easy BBQ Dip	BBQ or broiled quarters of yellow and green bell peppers		BBQ or broiled chicken drumsticks, spare ribs and sausages		
Sesame and Red Pepper Dip	blanched and chilled snow peas, baby sweet corn; celery and cucumber strips				rice and shrimp crackers
Sundried Tomato Stunner Dip	yellow, orange, red, green bell pepper strips			warm garlic bread	
Tapenade				toasted crusty bread, olive bread	
Tomato and Basil Dip	cucumber, celery, zucchini strips			breadsticks	
Tomato and Onion Sambal				pita bread strip	
Watercress and Yogurt Dip	crisp small lettuce leaves, celery and carrot strips	cooked crumb- or batter-coated salmon or white fish sticks			

BEAN AND LENTIL DIPS	ACCOMPANIMENTS				
	VEGETABLE	FRUIT	SEAFOOD	BREAD	SNACKS
Butter Bean Dip	carrot strips, broccoli florets, blanched fine green beans		fish sticks or scampi		
Creamed Chickpea and Hazelnut Dip	celery and cucumber strips	cored apple wedges			potato chips
Curried Bean Dip				pita bread strips, crusty bread	
Green Lentil and Spinach Dip	bell pepper strips			pita bread strips	
Hot Tex Mex Dip	bell pepper strips				tortilla chips, taco shells
Hummus	peppers, celery, cucumber strips			pita bread strips	
Mexican Bean Dip	red, yellow, green bell pepper strips				tortilla chips
Pesto Bean Dip	tomato wedges			breadsticks, cubed crusty bread, olive bread	
Red Lentil Dal	celery and cucumber strips			warm strips of pita bread, crusty bread	

SAVORY FRUIT DIPS	ACCOMPANIMENTS					
	VEGETABLE	FRUIT	MEAT	BREAD	SNACKS	SWEETS
Apricot and Mango Chutney Dip	onion rings			crusty bread	samosas	
Cranberry and Orange Dip			crumb-coated turkey sticks – see page 52			
Curried Mango Dip	cucumber, red bell pepper strips			pita bread strips, crusty bread		
Papaya, Mango, and Pomegranate Salsa	wide strips of red, yellow, green bell peppers				tortilla chips	
Pineapple, Avocado, and Red Onion Salsa				pita bread strips	tortilla chips, nachos	
Pineapple and Chive Cheese Dip	celery, cucumber, carrot strips				selection of crackers	

SWEET FRUIT DIPS	ACCOMPANIMENTS					
	VEGETABLE	FRUIT	MEAT	BREAD	SNACKS	SWEETS
Autumnal Fruits with Port Dip		cored apple wedges				mini sweet muffins, lady fingers, marshmallows
Blueberry Swirl Dip		cored pear wedges				chocolate and vanilla cake
Butterscotch Dip		broiled bananas – see page 58				
Cinnamon and Raisin Yogurt Dip		apple fritters – see recipe on page 57				
Kiwi Cream Dip		wedges of mango, papaya, banana				
Strawberry Dream Dip		wedges of pear, peach, banana				marshmallows, mini doughnuts, mini sweet muffins

MORE FAVORITES	ACCOMPANIMENTS					
	VEGETABLE	FRUIT	SEAFOOD	MEAT	BREAD	SNACKS
Caper and Gherkin Dip	red, yellow, green bell pepper, zucchini and celery strips					
Creamy Egg Brunch Dip	tomato wedges		sliced smoked salmon rolled up into bite-sized pieces	cooked cocktail sausages, broiled smoked bacon strips	toast and crusty bread	
Egg and Parsley Dip					strips of white and brown toast	
Fresh Herbed Yogurt Dip	vegetable kabobs, strips of raw vegetables		fish kabobs	meat kabobs		
Garlic Dip	carrot, celery, bell pepper strips, broccoli and cauliflower florets					
Peppery Mayonnaise Dip	celery, carrot, cucumber, zucchini strips; blanched baby sweet corn					
Tahini Dip	celery strips	cored apple wedges				potato chips
Tofu and Peanut Butter Dip	strips of bell peppers				toasted bread strips	
Tofu and Sesame Dip	celery, cucumber, bell peppers, carrot strips, broccoli and cauliflower florets					
Whole-grain Mustard Dip	deep-fried baked batter-coated vegetables, e.g. onion rings, strips of eggplant and zucchini					

FONDUES	ACCOMPANIMENTS					
	VEGETABLE	FRUIT	SEAFOOD	MEAT	BREAD	SWEETS
Cider and Cheese Fondue	cucumber and celery chunks, tomato wedges	cored apple wedges		strips of cooked ham	cubed crusty bread	
Creamy Toffee Fondue						plain popcorn
Devil's Chocolate Fondue						cubed sponge cake, mini sweet muffins, mini doughnuts, cookies
Double Cheese Fondue	diced bell peppers, tomato wedges, sliced zucchini				cubed crusty bread, small breadsticks, cheese straws	
Fresh Tomato and Basil Fondue	diced bell peppers, celery chunks		shelled cooked jumbo shrimp		cubed crusty bread and garlic bread	
Marshmallow Delight Fondue		seedless grapes, sliced banana and peaches, strawberries				

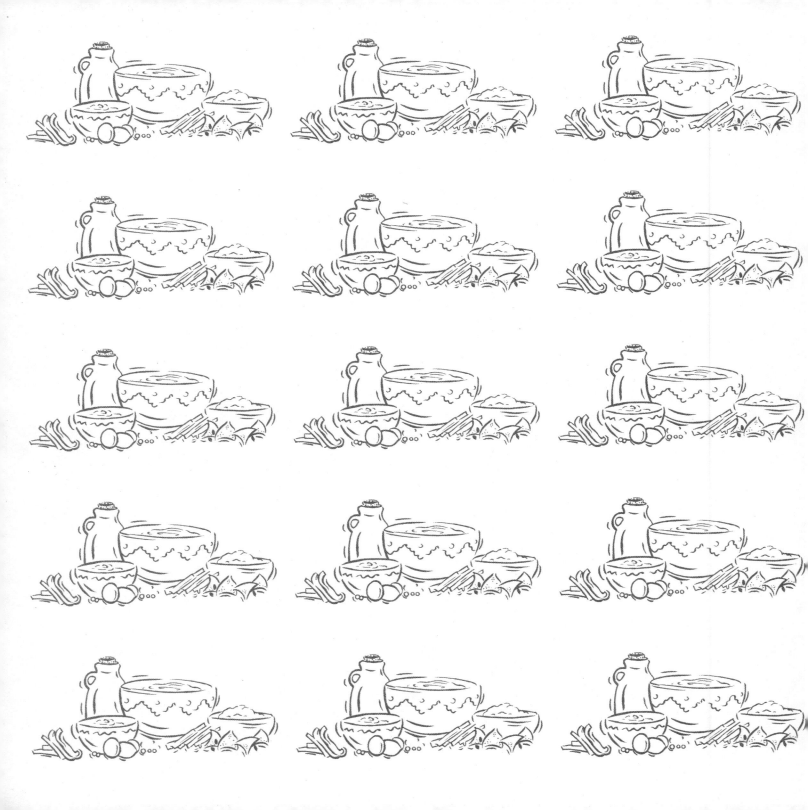